California Bar Examination

Performance Tests and Selected Answers

February 2015

The State Bar Of California
Committee of Bar Examiners/Office of Admissions

180 Howard Street • San Francisco, CA 94105-1639 • (415) 538-2300
845 S. Figueroa Street • Los Angeles, CA 90017-2515 • (213) 765-1500

PERFORMANCE TESTS AND SELECTED ANSWERS

FEBRUARY 2015

CALIFORNIA BAR EXAMINATION

This publication contains two performance tests from the February 2015 California Bar Examination and two selected answers for each test.

The answers were assigned high grades and were written by applicants who passed the examination after one read. The answers were produced as submitted by the applicant, except that minor corrections in spelling and punctuation were made for ease in reading. They are reproduced here with the consent of the authors.

CONTENTS

February 2015

California
Bar
Examination

Performance Test A
INSTRUCTIONS AND FILE

IN RE VIRTA AND BURNSEN

IN RE VIRTA AND BURNSEN

INSTRUCTIONS

1. This performance test is designed to evaluate your ability to handle a select number of legal authorities in the context of a factual problem involving a client.

2. The problem is set in the fictional State of Columbia, one of the United States.

3. You will have two sets of materials with which to work: a File and a Library.

4. The File contains factual materials about your case. The first document is a memorandum containing the instructions for the tasks you are to complete.

5. The Library contains the legal authorities needed to complete the tasks. The case reports may be real, modified, or written solely for the purpose of this performance test. If the cases appear familiar to you, do not assume that they are precisely the same as you have read before. Read each thoroughly, as if it were new to you. You should assume that cases were decided in the jurisdictions and on the dates shown. In citing cases from the Library, you may use abbreviations and omit page citations.

6. You should concentrate on the materials provided, but you should also bring to bear on the problem your general knowledge of the law. What you have learned in law school and elsewhere provides the general background for analyzing the problem; the File and Library provide the specific materials with which you must work.

7. Although there are no restrictions on how you apportion your time, you should probably allocate at least 90 minutes to reading and organizing before you begin preparing your response.

8. Your response will be graded on its compliance with instructions and on its content, thoroughness, and organization.

CLARK, MACHADO & SAMUELIAN

Attorneys at Law

<u>MEMORANDUM</u>

TO: Applicant

FROM: Dario Machado, Managing Partner

SUBJECT: Richard Burnsen and B-G Investors

DATE: February 24, 2015

      I met with Chris Conner on short notice. Conner is a junior partner in our firm, specializing in transactional law. He is in the middle of closing a stock purchase deal for our clients, Richard Burnsen and Burnsen-Goldman Investors ("B-G"), and must decide immediately whether to close the deal and transfer the stock certificates. The seller is trying to revoke, and his counsel insists that Conner has become the escrow holder of the transaction. His counsel also says that if Conner does not return the stock certificates, they would sue Conner and our firm.

      We have two interrelated problems: Are there any ethical or fiduciary issues raised by Conner's actions, and what does Conner do now? Please draft an objective memorandum analyzing these two problems, organized in two parts, specifically addressing the issues listed below.

Part I - <u>Ethical / Fiduciary Issues</u>.

A. Did Conner become an escrow holder for all the parties?

B. If Conner acted as an escrow holder, was it proper for him to be an attorney for one party and an escrow holder for all parties?

C. If Conner acted in this dual capacity, does it restrict his ability both to advise his clients and to follow their instructions?

D. If Conner is an escrow holder, what are his duties to the opposing party?

Part II - <u>Options</u>.

Listed below are the options that I want to consider at this moment. Analyze the consequences and legal exposure of Conner and the firm resulting from each option. Finally, recommend which option best serves our firm's interests.

1. Complete the purchase and forward stock certificates for transfer.
2. File an interpleader action against our clients and the seller.
3. Do nothing immediately and retain possession of the stock certificates, until seller sues or parties work out a settlement.

At this point consider only the potential liability of Conner and our firm. Someone else in the firm will focus on our clients' risks.

Dario Machado Meeting with Christopher Conner

February 24, 2015

MACHADO: Okay, Chris, let me turn on the tape recorder. From what you've already told me it's obvious that one of our associates is going to have to look into this matter immediately and will need to know what's happened.

CONNER: Let me give you the deal in a nutshell. As I told you, our firm represents Richard Burnsen, founder, CEO, and majority shareowner of BTI. That's Burnsen Technologies, Inc. BTI develops and markets bio-compact discs for clinical diagnostics. It began as a small company operated out of Burnsen's house, but grew much larger, now has 60 employees, and occupies a large suite in New Bennett, Columbia.

Jordan Virta helped start BTI and had been the chief scientist and a vice president. At the start of the year, Virta and Burnsen had a falling out, and Virta resigned. At the time Virta held 2,000,000 shares of BTI stock that he had received in exchange for the assignment of all of his patents and inventions. But, even though he quit, Virta was still subject to a consulting agreement that gave BTI the rights to his future inventions for 2 years after he left BTI. Virta needed cash and to get back to work. Virta began discussing a sale of his stock to Burnsen.

MACHADO: So what was the deal?

CONNER: At the beginning of this year, Burnsen proposed to buy 2,000,000 of Virta's shares for $1.50 per share. Virta would receive $500,000 on signing the stock purchase agreement, and Burnsen would execute a promissory note payable to Virta over the next 2 years, secured by the shares. Burnsen thought it was a good deal, since last year, some other investors had paid as much as $5.00 per share of BTI stock.

MACHADO: Why the low price?

CONNER: Because Burnsen offered, as part of the transaction, to cancel the consulting agreement that was hindering Virta's ability to work elsewhere. The deal was delayed because Burnsen couldn't come up with the down payment. But then Burnsen brought in another investor, Gerald Goldman, to help buy the Virta stock. We formed a company called Burnsen-Goldman Investors -- B-G, for short. Then on behalf of B-G, I negotiated a stock purchase agreement and a promissory note with Virta's attorney, Steven Dunn.

MACHADO: Did the stock purchase agreement include canceling the old consulting agreement that had granted BTI control of Virta's future inventions?

CONNER: Oh, yeah. That was a critical part, along with the terms of transfer of the shares themselves. Virta insisted on payment first.

MACHADO: What were those terms?

CONNER: That the deal would only close after the purchase agreement and promissory note were signed and after Virta acknowledged receipt of the down payment of $500,000. After the deal closed, then Virta's signed share certificates would go to BTI's transfer agent to be reissued in B-G's name. The shares would then go into an escrow account at Columbia State Bank and Trust Company, as security for the note, and thereafter be distributed by the Trust Company to B-G only as it paid for the shares according to the payment schedule.

MACHADO: Is this in writing?

CONNER: The escrow at the trust company? Yeah, Columbia State Bank and Trust Company's instructions were that it would hold all the shares, and release them to B-G as they made the down payment and the 5 payments of $500,000 provided under the note.

MACHADO: Who has the share certificates now?

CONNER: I do.

MACHADO: How did that come about?

CONNER: A few days ago, on February 16th, Dunn and I finished drafting the documents, but it turned out that Dunn was leaving for a couple of weeks on vacation and wouldn't be available for an office closing. Instead, we agreed to do it by mail. Exchange the signed documents, make the down payment, and then transfer shares to escrow.

MACHADO: Was this an oral agreement between you and Dunn or in writing?

CONNER: Both. We said that I'd hold the documents until everyone signed and Virta had confirmed he had the down payment. I think that's what our letters say too.

MACHADO: Let me get this straight. You were to hold the share certificates until the deal closes?

CONNER: Right.

MACHADO: Did Dunn do his part, get Virta to sign the stock purchase agreement and stock certificates?

CONNER: Yeah. I got all that on February 17th, hand-delivered, along with Dunn's letter. That's when the trouble started. I gave the agreement and promissory note to Burnsen for him and Goldman to sign. At first, I didn't hear anything, but on the 18th and 19th of February I start getting calls from Virta asking why the deposit hadn't been made into his account, and demanding that the deal close on February 18th as agreed. I started leaving messages for Burnsen to call me. On February 20th Burnsen called me and said that he and Goldman wanted me to move the closing back to February 23rd, and that they wanted to move back the payment schedule on the promissory note. Since Dunn was unavailable, Burnsen and Goldman were dealing directly with Virta.

MACHADO: What happened?

CONNER: Both Burnsen and Goldman talked to Virta, quite a few times, in the next couple of days. Virta was adamant that he wanted the down payment and for the deal to close immediately. Even though they had missed the original closing date, Virta was still expecting the deal to close; at least that's what they told me.

MACHADO: Did Virta agree to revise the payment schedule?

CONNER: Burnsen and Goldman weren't clear on that. Sometimes they'd report that he agreed or, at least, he didn't disagree to change the payment schedule. They did say he objected that the new schedule would put 4 rather than 3 payments in a single year, and make the tax bite too much.

MACHADO: So, the payment terms were critical to Virta?

CONNER: That's what he said to them. I think he has always doubted Burnsen's and Goldman's ability to come up with the down payment and make the payments. Frankly, it was a fair concern. Burnsen and Goldman were betting that BTI's growth would spin off enough for them to pay off Virta.

MACHADO: What did you think?

CONNER: You know, I really don't know. We don't ask clients for financial statements. Burnsen totally believed in his company. And Goldman? For all I know, he refinanced his house to come up with the down payment for Virta.

MACHADO: Very well. With what they told you, what did you do?

CONNER: I told them that I'd write up an amended promissory note and that they should come in and sign it, as well as the stock purchase agreement that they still hadn't signed. But, before they did, Burnsen called me at home, on the night of February 22nd, and read me a notice of revocation of the offer that Virta had faxed him that evening. We scheduled a conference call including Goldman for 10:00 p.m. that night.

MACHADO: What happened on the conference call?

CONNER: Goldman and Burnsen wanted to go ahead with the purchase, at least on their terms. Goldman agreed to deposit the $500,000, if it could close the deal on their terms.

MACHADO: What did you advise?

CONNER: That we probably did not have a defensible basis to go ahead and close. I told them that I'd make the best arguments I could, but that they shouldn't expect a miracle.

MACHADO: Were there colorable arguments?

CONNER: Some. The closing date was never ironclad. Even Virta demanded we close after the date had passed. We had an argument that the payment schedule had been amended orally. Also, the agreement didn't have a time-is-of-the-essence clause, and we could argue that the new payment schedule wasn't a substantive change.

MACHADO: So, you didn't think it should be a deal breaker?

CONNER: Perhaps not. Burnsen and Goldman believed that if we put the $500,000 down payment in Virta's hands, he'd see that they were going ahead, and he could be persuaded to accept the amended payment schedule. And if we closed, then the onus would be on Virta to challenge the executed deal. A little pressure like that might do it. Besides, by that point, Burnsen and Goldman had decided that the original payment schedule was unrealistic, and they couldn't have met it.

MACHADO: Did you think pushing the revised deal was a risk?

CONNER: No, just the usual give-and-take that goes on to finish the last details of a deal. Nothing more than aggressive representation of a client, I'd call it. An unrealistic payment schedule wasn't in Virta's interest either.

MACHADO: Well, okay. Is that what was agreed on the conference call?

CONNER: Yeah. Next morning, Goldman deposited the $500,000 into Virta's account. Here's the deposit slip he brought us, February 23rd at 9:52 a.m., and we faxed it to Virta and Dunn immediately. Do you want the deposit slip?

MACHADO: No, just keep it in the file. What happened next?

CONNER: I drafted a new promissory note, with the payment schedule Burnsen and Goldman wanted. They came in and signed the stock purchase agreement that Virta had already signed and I'd been holding, and they also signed the new promissory note.

MACHADO: The new payment schedule was not set forth in the stock purchase agreement?

CONNER: No. The payment schedule was only in the promissory note, and the stock purchase agreement provided that payments were to be made as provided in the promissory note. So we could use and sign the agreement that Virta had already signed. Then, that same afternoon, yesterday, I delivered a letter to Virta and Dunn confirming that the deal was ready to close and I was going to transmit the documents.

MACHADO: Why to Virta?

CONNER: Everybody had agreed that all parties should be copied on documents where appropriate. But this morning I received a call from another lawyer in Dunn's firm, a Russell Taylor, threatening to sue me if I transfer the shares.

MACHADO: Have you sent the shares for transfer?

CONNER: No, I haven't. I still have the share certificates, right here in the file.

MACHADO: Did you tell that to Taylor?

CONNER: Yes, but I certainly led him to believe that I was going ahead to close, you know, as my clients wanted, to pressure and to shift the burden to Virta.

MACHADO: Would it now be a problem if you had to back off, should we decide it's necessary?

CONNER: Probably embarrassing, but overall, not that bad.

MACHADO: Okay. What did you say to him?

CONNER: First, to chill, relax. Transferring the stock certificates wasn't a big deal, nor an irrevocable step. I reminded him that Virta had a specific remedy under the Commercial Code. Section 8403 permits suits to stop the transfer agent from registering the change of ownership. I urged him, instead of that, though, to work positively and finish the deal. The original deal was still on the table. Virta had a half a million dollars in his hands. A little more taxes next year isn't anything compared to that and absolutely trivial compared to Virta's ability to get back to work. I even suggested that they should calculate the additional tax burden of the amended payment schedule and make a counteroffer, adding it to the selling price. It couldn't be more than a few pennies per share.

MACHADO: Did it persuade him?

CONNER: No. Taylor said that I'm responsible as the escrow agent, and that the deal had been revoked. The shares must be returned or they would hold us responsible for the full, present value of the shares.

MACHADO: Sounds like he's claiming that would make the firm liable for money that our clients may not have?

CONNER: Exactly. That's what made me stop and realize I needed to discuss our options with a senior member of the firm.

MACHADO: What about returning the certificates?

CONNER: That's the bind. My clients don't want me to return the shares. They were explicit on that. They want to complete the purchase and believe that transferring the shares to BTI for reissuance in their name helps them. My duty to my clients comes first, even if Taylor claims I'm an escrow agent.

MACHADO: Was that claim a surprise?

CONNER: Yeah. I don't see how they can claim that I became their escrow agent. I didn't volunteer to be their agent. I didn't do anything unusual for a transactional attorney. We do that all the time, hold the documents until everyone signs and the money is deposited, then distribute as everyone agreed. It's like an escrow, I guess, but it doesn't trump my duty of loyalty to my client. They seem to be saying that it's improper to be both a lawyer for a party and act as the escrow, if that's what I was. If so, the option of having to withdraw as counsel would be hard to accept.

MACHADO: If you're deemed to be an escrow agent, another option would be that you could interplead both sides of the dispute and deposit the share certificates in court, right?

CONNER: Sue my own clients? It is not in my clients' best interests for me to sue them and force them to hire another lawyer to defend themselves against me. How can that be consistent with my duty of loyalty to my clients?

MACHADO: Granted, that seems antithetical to everything we believe and do as lawyers.

CONNER: Seems to me that I don't have a choice but to follow my clients' instructions, and send the certificates to the BTI transfer agent. True, the transfer agent will change ownership to B-G, but really B-G only gets the shares they've paid for with the $500,000 down payment, and the remainder goes to the Trust Company and is held and released only as B-G makes future payments. Virta's not harmed by the closing and the transfer. Besides, as I told Taylor, Section 8403 is the functional equivalent of an interpleader. The results of a suit under Section 8403 and an interpleader are the same. The stock remains in Virta's name and under the control of a judge pending resolution of the dispute. Either way, Virta doesn't get and can't sell the stock until it's decided. The only difference is that Virta files the lawsuit instead of us.

MACHADO: Perhaps. I think the question is, which is the right course of action? Leave me the key documents and we'll get together shortly.

CONNER: Thanks. See you soon.

CLARK, MACHADO & SAMUELIAN

Attorneys at Law

Parkside, Columbia

February 16, 2015

HAND-DELIVERED

Steven J. Dunn
Dunn and Jaime
12 Main Street, Suite 100
Riverton, Columbia

Dear Steve:

Enclosed are the stock purchase agreement and promissory note that we have finished drafting. Since you will be on vacation after tomorrow, I propose that we have the documents executed by our respective clients, and close by mail. The following steps should permit us to close on February 18, 2015.

First, all parties will execute the documents and return all signed copies to me so that I have them on Wednesday, February 18, 2015. I shall then distribute those copies to the appropriate parties on that day. Steve, if you send me the stock certificates representing all of the pledged shares, with stock powers duly executed by Dr. Virta, I undertake to hold them until I have the agreement, together with the promissory note, executed by B-G Investors, at which time I shall send the promissory note to you and the share certificates to BTI for transfer and reissuance in B-G's name and delivery to Columbia State Bank and Trust Company.

I envy your Florida vacation during our annual monsoon season.

Sincerely,

/s/ Chris Conner

Christopher C. Conner

cc: Richard Burnsen

        Gerald Goldman

        Dr. Jordan Virta

DUNN and JAIME

Attorneys at Law
Riverton, Columbia

February 17, 2015

Christopher C. Conner

Clark, Machado & Samuelian

605 First Street, Suite 810

Parkside, Columbia

Dear Chris:

This will confirm that we have completed the documents to close the sale to B-G Investors of 2 million of Dr. Jordan Virta's shares on February 18, 2015. I have enclosed the following documents, all duly executed and signed by Dr. Virta:

1. A stock purchase agreement.
2. A promissory note.
3. The original stock certificates with executed stock assignments for 2,000,000 shares in Burnsen Technologies, Inc. (BTI).

These documents are all delivered to you to be held by you until both of the following conditions are satisfied:

(a) You have signed copies of all of the above-referenced documents and are authorized to deliver to me the originals of all such documents; and

(b) Dr. Virta has confirmed that the $500,000 has been deposited into his bank account.

Upon satisfaction of these conditions, the sale shall close, and only on satisfaction of these conditions are you authorized to send the share certificates to BTI for reissuance in B-G's name. Either you or BTI then is authorized to transfer the shares to Columbia State Bank and Trust Company, pursuant to the formal escrow instructions on file with the Trust Company.

Sincerely,

/s/ Steven J. Dunn

Steven J. Dunn

cc: Dr. Jordan Virta

Richard Burnsen and Gerald Goldman

FAX

Dr. Jordan Virta

TO: Richard Burnsen and Gerald Goldman, B-G Investors

SUBJECT: Revocation of Offer to Sell Stock

DATE: February 22, 2015

Dear Richard and Gerald:

I am out of patience. You are out of time.

We had agreed that this transaction would close on February 18, 2015. On that date you and your counsel had all of the documents, and all of the documents had been signed by me and approved by your counsel.

I have been calling my bank several times a day to learn if the down payment has been deposited as promised. It is now 4 days later, and no deposit. I don't know if you ever signed the agreement or the promissory note. I have never received signed copies of the documents.

Instead, each of you has been asking for an extension of the date of closing to February 23, 2015, and for a new, unacceptable payment schedule.

Each of these is a material breach of the agreement, if you ever signed it.

Effective this moment, I do hereby withdraw my offer to sell my shares in BTI.

I hereby demand that you and all agents and counsel acting on your behalf immediately return to me my stock certificates and all documents delivered by me.

Very truly yours,

/s/ Jordan Virta

Jordan Virta, Ph.D.

cc: Steven J. Dunn
      Christopher C. Conner

CLARK, MACHADO & SAMUELIAN

Attorneys at Law

Parkside, Columbia

February 23, 2015

HAND-DELIVERED

Steven J. Dunn

Dunn and Jaime

12 Main Street, Suite 100

Riverton, Columbia

Dear Steven:

It is my understanding that, in separate conversations with Messrs. Burnsen and Goldman, Dr. Virta has urged that the transaction close immediately and agreed to accept these deliveries today.

It is my further understanding that the two conditions to close and release the stock certificates set forth in your letter of February 17, 2015 have been fully satisfied, to wit: (a) I have copies of the Stock Purchase Agreement, signed by all the parties, and of the Promissory Note, dated February 23, 2015, signed by Messrs. Burnsen and Goldman, the parties to be bound; and (b) I have a deposit slip confirming that $500,000 has been deposited into Dr. Virta's bank account.

Thus, we have completed the sale of Dr. Virta's shares in Burnsen Technologies, Inc. (BTI), and the transaction is now ready to close. Accordingly, I will send Dr. Virta's stock certificates that we received from you to BTI's transfer agent for transfer of ownership of the shares on BTI's books to B-G Investors, issuance of the appropriate renamed share certificates and transfer to Columbia State Bank and Trust Company.

Please find enclosed your copy of the fully executed Stock Purchase Agreement and the amended Promissory Note, signed by Messrs. Burnsen and Goldman.

Sincerely,

/s/ Chris Conner

Christopher C. Conner

cc: Jordan Virta, with all copies, and also hand-delivered this date

DUNN and JAIME

Attorneys at Law
Riverton, Columbia

February 24, 2015

VIA FAX

Christopher C. Conner
Clark, Machado & Samuelian
605 First Street, Suite 810
Parkside, Columbia

Dear Mr. Conner:

On behalf of our client, Dr. Jordan Virta, I hereby demand that you stop all efforts purporting to close the transaction for the disposition of Dr. Virta's shares in BTI.

There never was a signed agreement. Your clients never accepted the agreement that Dr. Virta signed; it did not close on February 18, 2015, as had been agreed, and your clients never performed the conditions. It never took effect.

Any action on your part to divest Dr. Virta of his stock is a conversion and a breach of your fiduciary duty as the escrow agent of the parties. The only course of action that will avoid liability is to return Dr. Virta's share certificates immediately.

We are astonished that any attempt would be made to exercise dominion and control over Dr. Virta's stock certificates in light of his revocation of the stock purchase offer and cancellation of the transaction. Please take notice that, if you do not immediately return Mr. Virta's stock certificates and related documents, you and your law firm will face significant personal liability for the tort of conversion, having exercised dominion and control over the stock certificates.

Today Dr. Virta received notice from his bank that $500,000 was deposited in his account on February 23, 2015. As soon as he is notified that the funds are at his disposal, Dr. Virta will return the entire $500,000 by immediate wire transfer to Messrs. Burnsen and Goldman.

Sincerely,

/s/ J. Russell Taylor

J. Russell Taylor

February 2015

California
Bar
Examination

Performance Test A
LIBRARY

IN RE VIRTA AND BURNSEN

LIBRARY

SELECTED PROVISIONS OF COLUMBIA CODE OF CIVIL PROCEDURE, COLUMBIA COMMERCIAL CODE, AND COLUMBIA PROFESSIONAL CODE

Columbia Code of Civil Procedure

Section 386. Interpleader

Any person, firm, corporation, association or other entity against whom double or multiple claims are made, or may be made, by two or more persons which are such that they may give rise to double or multiple liability, may bring an action against the claimants to compel them to interplead and litigate their several claims. When the person, firm, corporation, association or other entity against whom such claims are made, or may be made, is a defendant in an action brought upon one or more of such claims, it may file a cross-complaint in interpleader.

Columbia Commercial Code

Section 8403.

(a)   A person who is a registered owner of corporate shares may serve a written demand that the issuer of corporate shares not register an improper or unauthorized transfer of the shares.

(b)   The issuer of the corporate shares may withhold registration of the transfer for a period of time, not to exceed 30 days, in order to provide the person who initiated the demand an opportunity to obtain legal process.

(c)   A person who is the registered owner of corporate shares may seek an appropriate order, injunction, or other process from a court of competent jurisdiction enjoining the issuer of the corporate shares from registering an improper or unauthorized transfer of the shares.

Columbia Professional Code

Section 17002.

(a) It shall be unlawful for any person to engage in business as an escrow agent within this state except by means of a corporation duly organized for that purpose and licensed by the Commissioner of Corporations as an escrow agent.

(b) It shall not be unlawful for any person to engage in the business of an escrow agent, without authorization or license by the Commissioner of Corporations, if the person is:

    (1) Doing business under any law of this state or the United States relating to banks, trust companies, building and loan or savings and loan associations, or insurance companies.

    (2) Licensed to practice law in Columbia who has a bona fide client relationship with a principal in a real estate or personal property transaction and who is not actively engaged in the business of an escrow agent.

    (3) Licensed by the Real Estate Commissioner while performing acts in the course of or incidental to a real estate transaction in which the broker is an agent or a party to the transaction and in which the broker is performing an act for which a real estate license is required.

Section 17003.

"Escrow" means any transaction in which one person, for the purpose of effecting the sale, transfer, encumbering, or leasing of real or personal property to another person, delivers any written instrument, money, evidence of title to real or personal property, or other thing of value to a third person to be held by that third person until the happening of a specified event or the performance of a prescribed condition, when it is then to be delivered by that third person to a grantee, grantor, promisee, promisor, obligee, obligor, bailee, bailor, or any agent or employee of any of the latter.

WASMAN v. SEIDEN

Columbia Court of Appeal (1998)

Does an attorney have a duty to safeguard property entrusted to him during settlement negotiations by an adverse party? Yes.

Plaintiff Kenneth Wasman sued his ex-wife and others for torts allegedly arising out of a marital dissolution gone awry. One of the named defendants was an attorney who arranged the property settlement on behalf of the wife. As to the causes of action against this attorney, the trial court sustained a general demurrer without leave to amend. Wasman appeals from the ensuing judgment of dismissal. We reverse.

Wasman alleged, and we assume for purposes of review, the following facts. Kenneth and Barbara Wasman married in 1992, and separated in 1995. In 1996, Barbara hired attorney Charles Schwenck to dissolve the marriage. The parties agreed to bifurcate the proceedings, with an immediate dissolution of the marriage contingent on acceptance of a proposed division of marital property, to be "formalized" later. The terms of the property division included Kenneth's conveyance to Barbara of his community interest in a Newport Beach residence in exchange for $70,000 in cash or a promissory note in that amount secured by a grant deed on the property.

In October 1996, Barbara, now married to Schwenck, retained new counsel, Peter Seiden, to complete the marital property settlement. After counsel conferred many times by phone, Kenneth's attorney Jeffrey Hartman sent a letter to Seiden enclosing a final draft of the settlement agreement and a grant deed conveying the Newport Beach property to Barbara. Kenneth had executed both documents. The letter stated that Seiden was "authorized to record the deed only upon obtaining" for Kenneth the $70,000 in cash or the promissory note.

Hartman received no response to his letter. Over the next few months he telephoned Seiden several times to ask the status of the settlement agreement. Hartman subsequently learned that Barbara, without handing over the cash or promissory note, had obtained the grant deed from Seiden and recorded it.

Kenneth Wasman sued Peter Seiden for legal malpractice. Seiden's general demurrer to the complaint was sustained.

The central issue in this appeal is whether Seiden had a legal duty to safeguard the executed grant deed until Barbara satisfied the condition of its delivery. Wasman argues Seiden owed him a professional duty to guard the deed until the stated condition for recordation was met; he contends breach of that duty was legal malpractice. But the law of professional negligence does not supply the foundation necessary for the duty Wasman asserts here.

We have rejected the theory that attorneys owe a duty of care to adverse third parties in litigation. Only in the limited circumstances when third parties are the intended beneficiaries of an attorney's services are they entitled to bring actions for professional negligence. Wasman's attempt to bring himself within this exception by arguing he was an intended beneficiary of the marital settlement is patently absurd: The agreement resulted from arm's-length negotiations between counsel acting to protect their respective clients' interests.

Although Seiden owed Wasman no professional duty, his acceptance of Wasman's deed would give rise to a duty of care. The wellspring of this duty is the fiduciary role of an escrow holder. An escrow is created when, for the purpose of facilitating a transaction, property is delivered to an escrow holder to be held until the conditions specified in agreed-upon instructions are fulfilled, when the property is to be delivered to another according to the instructions. See Professional Code, Section 17003.

The threshold issue in this appeal, then, is whether the complaint sufficiently alleges the elements of an escrow.

Wasman variously alleges in the complaint that Seiden "undertook to exercise reasonable care to protect Plaintiff's Deed" and "voluntarily accepted the trust and confidence reposed in him with regard to Plaintiff's Grant Deed." Significantly, there is no allegation of an express undertaking by Seiden or of agreed-upon instructions; rather, Wasman infers acceptance of the entrustment from the attorney's failure to reject or otherwise respond to the deed's delivery.

We find this a permissible inference. According to allegations in the complaint, the parties had successfully concluded settlement discussions. The final agreement had been reduced to writing and executed by Wasman; the document lacked only

Barbara's signature. The remaining acts required by the agreement were Wasman's conveying his interest in the Newport Beach property to Barbara, and her transferring to him a note or cash in the amount of $70,000. Given this state of affairs, Wasman's delivery of the grant deed to Seiden along with the executed settlement agreement can only be seen as a good faith attempt to facilitate settlement. The act appears foolish only when viewed against a backdrop of unethical and unprofessional practices by some attorneys.

Wasman and his attorney Hartman reasonably relied on Seiden because of his professional status and role as attorney for Barbara. If Seiden did not want to be responsible for the deed, he should have promptly returned it to Wasman. We hold a trier of fact could find any failure to do so was an acceptance of Wasman's entrustment and of its conditions. Thus, the allegations of acceptance are legally sufficient.

Having accepted the deed from Wasman, Seiden was bound to comply strictly with the escrow instructions. Specifically, he was obligated to prevent recordation of the deed until Barbara deposited into escrow the sum due to Wasman. Violation of an escrow instruction gives rise to an action for breach of contract; similarly, negligent performance by an escrow holder creates liability in tort for breach of duty.

Wasman forgoes the contract claim and alleges negligence in Seiden's handling of the deed. These allegations of negligence, however, are not the stuff of which legal malpractice claims are made. An attorney's failure to prevent a client's unauthorized seizure and recordation of a document held in escrow is not lawyering. But Wasman's erroneous labeling of his cause of action as one for professional negligence is of no consequence. To withstand a general demurrer, a complaint need only state some cause of action from which liability results.

Seiden's liability is not founded upon professional negligence, but under the duty as a bailee to keep the property and not dispose of it without the authority of the depositor. Although not expressly pleaded, we believe the facts alleged are sufficient to state a cause of action for conversion. Conversion is the wrongful exercise of dominion over the property of another. The general rule is that the foundation for the action of conversion rests neither in the knowledge nor the intent of the defendant. It rests upon the unwarranted interference by defendant with the dominion over the property of the plaintiff from which injury to the latter results. Therefore, good or bad faith, care or negligence, and knowledge or ignorance, are ordinarily immaterial.

The elements of a conversion claim are: (1) the plaintiff's ownership or right to possession of the property; (2) the defendant's conversion by a wrongful act or disposition of property rights; and (3) damages. As a general rule, the normal measure of damages for conversion is the value of the property at the time of the conversion and a fair compensation for the time and money properly expended in pursuit of the property (Civil Code, Section 3336).

The misdelivery of entrusted property of another constitutes a conversion of it even though he acted innocently and by mistake.

Seiden argues that saddling lawyers with the obligations of escrow holders will expose them to third party tort liability simply for helping clients conclude transactions and litigation. We do not intend to discourage attorneys from facilitating transactions or settlements. Indeed, it is both useful and commonplace to entrust attorneys with closing documents, settlement agreements, releases, funds and other items. However, we caution that an attorney cannot convert the escrowed property to his or her client's own use.

The court erred in sustaining the general demurrer to this cause of action.

The judgment is reversed.

DIAZ V. UNITED COLUMBIA BANK

Columbia Court of Appeal (1977)

Plaintiff and appellant Edelso Diaz executed a written agreement for the sale of his assets in the La Lechonera Restaurant to Antonio Gil. Diaz was a recent immigrant and could not read or write English and was ignorant of legal formalities. The agreement was prepared by a notary public and provided that the total purchase price was $19,000, payable by a promissory note payable by installments of $300. In furtherance of the sale, an escrow was opened by Antonio Gil at the United Columbia Bank ("Bank"). The escrow was processed on printed forms of the Bank signed by Edelso Diaz and by Antonio Gil. The original escrow instructions provided for a "note for $7,000 executed by Antonio Gil, in favor of Edelso Diaz, principal payable $200 or more per month and continuing until paid." Later, the escrow was supplemented by an additional instruction, also on a Bank form, as follows: "You are hereby instructed to reduce the principal amount of the note for $7,000 being delivered through escrow by an amount of $2,000, representing costs of repairs paid by Antonio Gil, by endorsement on back of note, payable in installments of $200 on the first day of each month."

Prior to close of escrow, the Bank received a letter from an attorney, Jorge Fernandez Isla, representing the seller, Edelso Diaz. The letter stated that:

> NOTICE is hereby given that the amount indicated in above-referred escrow of seven thousand dollars ($7,000) is in error. The escrow instructions should have read "Note for $19,000" and not $7,000.

The letter enclosed the original sale agreement showing the actual selling price of $19,000.

Thereafter, disregarding the attorney's letter, the Bank deducted $2,000 from the $7,000, and prepared the note for $5,000. Gil signed the note, and the Bank closed the escrow.

Plaintiff Edelso Diaz seeks compensatory and punitive damages from defendants Gil and Bank. A demurrer was sustained without leave to amend as to the causes of action directed against the Bank.

The gravamen of the action against the defendant Bank lies in the claim that the escrow was improperly closed after the Bank received the attorney's letter notifying it of a claim of error with respect to the consideration for the sale as recited in the escrow instructions.

It is elemental that the fiduciary duty of an escrow holder is to comply strictly with the instructions of its principals and to exercise reasonable skill and ordinary diligence with respect to the employment. If the escrow holder fails to follow his instructions, he may be liable for any loss occasioned thereby.

It is, however, also elemental that, where the written escrow instructions amount to an agreement made by two principals with their joint agent and signed by both, neither can unilaterally change the instructions.

We therefore agree with defendant Bank that the escrow holder had no duty, contractual or otherwise, in the instant case to defer to plaintiff's unilateral notice as to the sale price and modify the escrow instructions in accordance therewith.

The question, however, remains as to the effect, if any, to be accorded the attorney's letter. While ineffective as a unilateral attempt to modify the instructions, it clearly placed the escrow holder on notice of a possible error in the instructions with respect to a material matter involving the escrow itself. The agreement of sale provided for a price of $19,000. The letter from attorney Isla not only advises of the total sale price as reflected in the agreement of sale, but specifically points out that the note should be for that amount ($19,000) rather than for $7,000. The failure of defendant Bank to heed the notice of a possible error in the escrow instructions and to close in the face thereof might be found to be a failure to exercise reasonable skill and ordinary diligence in the conduct of the escrow, and thus support recovery on a tort theory.

When faced with competing demands, an escrow holder must either hold the property or interplead it. The Bank neither held the property that was the subject of the sale nor interpleaded it. Its remarkable choice was to close escrow.

Section 386 of the Code of Civil Procedure permits a party against whom multiple claims are made to bring an interpleader action compelling the claimants to litigate their opposing claims. In an interpleader action, the court initially determines the right of the plaintiff to interplead the funds; if that right is sustained, an interlocutory decree is entered which requires the defendants to interplead and litigate their claims to the funds. Upon deposit of monies with the court, the plaintiff then may be discharged from liability and dismissed from the interpleader action. The effect of such an order is to preserve the fund, to discharge the stakeholder from further liability, and to keep the fund in the court's custody until the rights of the potential claimants of the monies can be adjudicated. By implementing an interpleader action and obtaining a discharge from further liability, the stakeholder avoids tort liability.

The Bank contends that it was not required to hold the property or interplead it, since neither party requested or sought those elections.

This argument presupposes two things. First, it assumes that there could have been no negotiated resolution of the matter, i.e., no new joint escrow instructions forthcoming, had the Bank simply not closed for a while to see how things played out. Second, it assumes that the litigation that ensued, once escrow had closed and Diaz was in the position of trying to undo it, was essentially the same as the litigation that would have ensued had an interpleader action been filed instead. We are not prepared to accept either assumption.

When the parties are still in escrow they tend to be predisposed to resolution. Once an escrow has been closed in such a manner as to make one party feel victimized and to force that party to hire a litigator to assert his or her rights, the chances of a speedy resolution diminish. There may even be a difference in the tenor of the litigation in that instance and in the instance in which a conflicted escrow holder has been the one to file an interpleader action.

Not surprisingly, the Bank cites no authority to the effect that closing an escrow is an acceptable alternative to holding the property or interpleading it. By definition, closing escrow, i.e., delivering property to parties on the completion of a transaction or the satisfaction of identified conditions, is not the same thing as filing an interpleader action, i.e., depositing property into the court until the rights thereto are resolved by judicial intervention. The former device harbors obvious dangers for an aggrieved party that the latter does not.

The Bank simply has not convinced us that putting the burden on a party to an escrow to commence immediate litigation following a premature closing is the same as the escrow holder's filing of an interpleader action before any closing takes place. In an interpleader action, the parties' rights remain protected while the court sorts things out. By filing an interpleader action, the conflicted escrow holder may shield himself or herself from liability, and protect the interests of the parties to the escrow as well. Interpleader is a safe harbor for the conflicted stakeholder. An escrow holder who fails to implead acts at his or her own peril.

While the Bank had an option to hold up or interplead, it did not have a right to ignore these options and blindly close the escrow without making a reasonable effort to determine the correctness of the instructions prepared by it on behalf of these illiterate parties. We conclude that a reasonable construction of the escrow instructions required the Bank, upon receipt of the Isla letter, to at least hold up closure until the situation was clarified. The nature and extent of the duty, its breach if any, and the effect thereof, must be resolved in the instant case as questions of fact and not as questions of law on demurrer.

Finally, the Bank contends that the prayer for punitive damages is improper. Civil Code section 3294 provides for the recovery of punitive damages "where it is proven by clear and convincing evidence that the defendant has been guilty of oppression, fraud, or malice. . . ." We have held that something more than the mere commission of a tort is always required for punitive damages. There must be circumstances of aggravation or outrage, such as spite or "malice," or a fraudulent or evil motive on the part of the defendant, or such a conscious and deliberate disregard of the interests of others that his conduct may be called willful or wanton.

The complaint alleged that, knowing full well that there was a dispute as to the terms of the escrow, the Bank closed it anyway. The Bank did so in complete disregard of the written notice from Diaz's attorney. The Bank did so while owing a duty, as escrow holder, to Diaz. There is sufficient evidence for a reasonable trier of fact to conclude by clear and convincing proof that the Bank acted in such a conscious and deliberate disregard for the rights of Diaz that its conduct could be characterized as willful or wanton, giving rise to a punitive damages award.

The order of dismissal is reversed.

PT-A: SELECTED ANSWER 1

MEMORANDUM

TO: Dario Machado

FROM: Applicant

SUBJECT: Richard Burnsen and B-G Investors

DATE: February 24, 2015

As per your request, the following is a memorandum addressing two over-arching questions regarding Richard Burnsen, B-G Investors, and Chris Conner: (1) What, if any, are the ethical or fiduciary issues raised by Conner's actions; and (2) what should Conner do now to best serve the firm's interest. The memo will address each question in turn.

Part I: Ethical and Fiduciary Duties
A. Did Conner become an escrow holder for all the parties?

The issue here is whether Conner did anything that made him into an escrow holder for both parties—B-G Investors *and* Virta. To answer that question, this section first discusses elements of "escrow," who may legally act as an escrow agent, and the necessary steps one takes to become an escrow agent.

Escrow is created when, "for the purpose of facilitating a transaction, property is delivered to an escrow holder to be held until the conditions specified in agreed-upon instructions are fulfilled, when the property is to be delivered to another according to the instructions." *Wasman v. Seiden* (1998) (citing Columbia Professional Code § 17003). One of the elements for creating escrow is the acceptance of the property by the escrow holder to fulfill his duties as escrow holder. But the acceptance of that role can be implied.

In *Wasman*, the plaintiff was the ex-husband in a divorce dispute. The parties had agreed to a settlement agreement that included the disposal of a piece of real property. The terms of the agreement called for transfer of the property to his ex-wife in exchange for $70,000 either in cash or a promissory note. The husband's lawyer mailed the wife's lawyer a final draft of the settlement agreement along with a grant deed conveying the property to the wife. The letter included instructions that the wife's lawyer was "authorized to record the deed only upon obtaining" for the husband the $70,000. When the wife took and recorded the deed—but failed to pay the $70,000—the husband brought suit against the wife's lawyer. The court found that the wife's lawyer was acting as an escrow holder for the husband, and as such owed him a duty of care.

The court held that the husband's lawyer "reasonably relied on [the wife's attorney] because of his professional status and role as attorney for [the wife]." *Wasman*. Furthermore, if the lawyer "did not want to be responsible for the deed, he should have promptly returned it to [the husband]." Because he did not, the lawyer "was bound to comply strictly with the escrow instructions," and any violation of this compliance gave rise to "an action for breach of contract," or tort for breach of duty.

Here, Conner states that he never volunteered to be Virta's agent, and that he didn't do anything unusual for a transaction attorney. And he does not believe that whatever it is he became vis-a-vis Virta, that shouldn't trump his responsibilities to his clients. But it appears that under *Wasman*, Conner did in fact become an escrow agent for all the parties. On Feb. 17, Dunn delivered to Conner a stock purchase agreement; a promissory note; and the original stock certificates, all executed and signed by Virta. When he delivered the documents and property—in the form of the stock certificates—he instructed Conner that they were to be "held" by him "until both of the following conditions are satisfied . . . ." He then listed the two conditions.

Like the plaintiff in Wasman, Dunn and Virta "reasonably relied" on Conner because of his professional status and role as attorney for B-G Investors. Moreover, if Conner did not want to be escrow agent, he should have returned the documents and property to Dunn. Because he did not do so, he is "bound to comply strictly with the escrow instructions." *Wasman*.

Nor does it matter—as Conner argues—that the real escrow agent is the Trust Company, which will only release the shares to B-G as they make their payments. There is still an escrow created under *Wasman* and CPC § 17003 for Conner to deliver the property to the Trust Company. The fact that the Trust Company will then act as an escrow agent is immaterial.

Thus, it appears that Conner did in fact become an escrow holder for all the parties.

B. If Conner acted as an escrow holder, was it proper for him to be an attorney for one party and an escrow holder for all parties?

Columbia law is clear that an attorney can also act as an escrow agent. Section 17002 of the Columbia Professional Code states that it is not unlawful for any person to engage in the business of an escrow agent—even without license or authorization—if that person is "[l]icensed to practice law in Columbia [and] has a bona fide client relationship with a principal in a real estate or personal property transaction and who is not actively engaged in the business of an escrow agent."

The court in *Wasman* specifically recognized an attorney who has all attending duties to his client must also act as an escrow agent with the attending duty of care to the party that delivered the property. In fact, the Wasman court admitted the dual-nature of this arrangement may be troubling for lawyers. Wasman. ("[The defendant] argues that saddling lawyers with the obligations of escrow holders will expose them to third-party tort liability simply for helping clients conclude transactions and litigation."). And the court acknowledged that "it is both useful and commonplace to entrust attorneys with closing documents, settlement agreements, releases, funds and other items." Wasman.

Nevertheless, the court was clear that once the escrow-agent relationship takes hold, the lawyer owes a duty of care to the party that delivered him the property.

Thus, it was proper for Conner to act as both attorney for one party and escrow holder for all parties, so long as he does not violate his duty of care that attached upon his becoming escrow holder.

C. If Conner acted in this dual capacity, does it restrict his ability both to advise his clients and to follow their instructions?

As discussed in the subsection above, nothing in law prohibits Conner from acting as his clients' attorney—and providing them with the advice they seek—as well as acting as an escrow holder for both parties. The conflict arises when his clients ask him to do something on their behalf that conflicts with his duties as escrow holder—the duties he owes to both parties.

As described in *Wasman*, "[a]n attorney's failure to prevent a client's unauthorized seizure and recordation of a document [there, a deed] held in escrow is not lawyering." *Wasman*. That is, where a client's demand is to take the property held in escrow even though the conditions have not yet been met for the client to legally take possession of it, the lawyer cannot properly follow their demand. The *Wasman* court held that that action would count as conversion—"the wrongful exercise of dominion over the property of another." Id.

Here, B-G wants to close—"at least on their terms," as Conner states. Conner, however, did not believe that he probably had a defensible basis to close, considering the fact that they wanted to change the payment schedule, and due to the fact that they were already past the closing date. Even though Conner believed he could make a few colorable arguments for the legality of his closing—the closing date was not "ironclad;" the payment schedule had been "amended orally; there was no time-is-of-the-essence clause—he still stated that closing probably was not defensible.

Conner is most likely correct in his assessment, especially as his "colorable arguments" are not that persuasive. (See below.) Certainly, Virta and his lawyers have disputed that the deal is ready to close in writing, which *Diaz v. United Columbia Bank* has held should "clearly place[] the escrow holder on notice of a possible error" in the closing of escrow. *Diaz*. And the failure of an escrow agent in such circumstances may be found to be a "failure to exercise reasonable skill and ordinary diligence in the conduct of the escrow." Id.

Thus, Conner may continue to advise his clients, but may not follow their instructions where they conflict the duties he owes all parties as escrow agent. Specifically, he should not presently close the deal.

D. If Conner is an escrow holder, what are his duties to the opposing party?

As discussed above, an escrow holder owes a "fiduciary duty" to "comply strictly with the instructions of its principals and to exercise reasonable skill and ordinary diligence with respect to the employment." *Diaz*. The *Wasman* Court agreed: "The wellspring of this duty is the fiduciary role of an escrow holder . . . . [The escrow holder is] bound to comply strictly with the escrow instructions."

Here, because Conner was acting as escrow holder for both parties, he owed Virta a fiduciary duty of care to comply with the instructions given to him by Virta when Virta deposited the property with Conner. The instructions that accompanied the delivery of the stock certificates to Conner included (i) a stock purchase agreement and (ii) a promissory note. The letter instructed Conner to hold on to the two documents, as well as the stock certificates, until "both of the following conditions are satisfied: (a) You have signed copies of all of the above-referenced documents and are authorized to deliver to me the originals of all such documents; and (b) Dr. Virta has confirmed that the $500,000 has been deposited into his bank account." Only after these conditions are met will the sale close. Then, Conner may send the stock certificates to BTI "for reissuance in B-G's name."

As *Wasman* instructs, Conner is bound "to comply strictly with the escrow instructions." This, he presently cannot do. The instructions clearly state that the deal will only close upon satisfaction of *both* conditions. Condition A requires that Conner sign copies of all the above-referenced documents, and deliver the originals to Dunn. But Conner's clients have redrafted the promissory note to include the amended payment schedule. Sending Virta the amended promissory note—even if it is signed by Conner's clients— does not "strictly" satisfy the instructions given to him as escrow holder.

Thus, Conner owes Virta the duty to strictly comply with his instructions, and cannot close the deal—and deliver the certificates to the Trust Company—with the amended promissory note.

Part II: Options.

The following section of the memo will analyze the consequences and legal exposure of Conner and the firm resulting from each listed option. Finally, the memorandum will recommend an option that best serves the firm's interests.

1. Complete the purchase and forward stock certificates for transfer.

Virta has made clear in his lawyer's Feb. 24 letter that if Conner closes and forwards the certificates for transfer, he will view that as a "conversion" and a "breach of his fiduciary duty," and Virta will likely sue under both contract and tort theories. Thus, there is a probable, immediate consequence that Conner will be sued if he forwards the certificates. The secondary issue is whether the suit will be successful.

Conversion

Conversion is "the wrongful exercise of dominion over the property of another." *Wasman*. There is a general rule that the plaintiff in a conversion suit does not need to prove the knowledge *or* intent of the defendant to make a prima facie case. The elements for this tort are: (i) the plaintiff's ownership or right to possession of the property; (ii) the defendant's conversion by a wrongful act or disposition of property rights; and (iii) damages. *Id.* As a general rule, the normal measure of damages for conversion is the "value of the property at the time of the conversion and a fair compensation for the time and money property expended in pursuit of the property." *Id.* (citing CC § 3336). Moreover, "[t]he misdelivery of entrusted property of another constitutes a conversion of it even though [the defendant] acted innocently and by mistake." *Wasman*. The *Wasman* Court finally warned that "an attorney cannot convert the escrowed property to his or her client's own use." *Id.*

Here, as discussed above, Conner was acting as an escrow holder for Virta's stock certificates. As such, he owes Virta a duty of care in his entrusted property. If he delivers that property to third party—here, the Trust Company—illicitly, Conner would be guilty of conversion under *Wasman* even if he acted innocently and by mistake. There is no scienter requirement for this tort, and no good-faith defense. Even if Conner believed that he could close the deal in good faith and deliver the certificates, if a court finds that he in fact "misdeliver[ed]" the certificates, he would be found guilty.

Moreover, damages for conversion is the value of the property at the time of conversion. This means that Conner—and by extension the firm—would be liable in damages to the amount that the stocks were actually worth when delivered to the Trust Company. The deal for the purchase of the stocks was at $1.50 a share, which is well below market price for the shares. Connor states that last year some investors had paid as much as $5 per share. Conner's and the firm's liability could easily reach $10,000,000 or more depending on the market value of the shares at the time Conner delivers them to the Trust Company.

Civil Code 3294 also allows for punitive damages "where it is proven by clear and convincing evidence that the defendant has been guilty of oppression, fraud, or malice . . . ." Here, Conner attempted to redraft the promissory note in violation of the instruction. A court may find that to be a fraudulent act and open up the possibility of punitive damages.

Thus, Virta will likely be successful in his conversion claim against Conner and the firm, and the liability may be exorbitant.

Breach of Fiduciary Duty

The escrow holder owes a fiduciary duty of care to person whose property he is holding. See *Wasman*. An "elemental" aspect of this duty requires the escrow holder to "comply strictly with the instructions of its principals and to exercise reasonable skill and ordinary diligence with respect to the employment." *Diaz*. A breach of this fiduciary duty "gives rise to an action for breach of contract." *Wasman*. Thus, if Virta is successful in his suit, he would likely get expectation damages—the market value of the shares minus the contract price. This could mean a large liability considering that the stocks are most likely selling for much more than the contract price of $1.50.

As discussed in subsection D of Part I, Virta's instructions clearly indicated that the deal could not close until the enclosed (i) stock purchase agreement and (ii) promissory note were signed and delivered back to Virta. Conner admits that he drafted a new promissory note that his clients signed because he needed to amend the payment schedule.

But this does not strictly comply with Virta's instructions. His condition clearly states that the enclosed promissory note must be signed and returned by Conner's clients in order for the deal to close. Substituting that note with a newly drafted one mostly likely counts as a breach of Conner's fiduciary duty to Virta—it does not comply strictly with his instructions. Moreover, Virta will most likely argue that his Feb. 22 letter and the Feb. 24 letter from his lawyers are even clearer statements of instructions for Conner not to close the deal and not to deliver the certificates. In fact, Virta attempts to rescind his offer to sell the shares to BTI entirely. As escrow holder, Conner is under a duty to comply with Virta's instructions.

Thus, Virta will likely be successful in his breach of fiduciary.

Section 8403

Conner seems to think it will be better for him and the firm if closes the deal and forces Virta to bring forth a Section 8493 action, which allows a registered owner of corporate shares to seek an injunction enjoining the issuer of the shares from registering an improper or unauthorized transfer of the shares. Conner states this is basically the same as an interpleader action, but it puts the onus on Virta, and it wouldn't require us to sue our own clients in an interpleader action.

But *Diaz* shows that courts look down on this strategy. In Diaz, the court said that "[w]hen the parties are still in escrow they tend to be predisposed to resolution. Once an escrow has been closed in such a manner to make one party feel victimized and to force that party to hire a litigator to assert his or her rights, the chances of a speedy resolution diminish." *Diaz*. The court concludes that the two paths—interpleading and forcing a Section 8403 action—are not the same. And reiterates, "An escrow holder who fails to implead acts at his or her own peril."

2. File an interpleader action against our clients and the seller.

In an interpleader action, "the parties' rights remain protected while the court sorts things out." *Diaz*. It allows the "conflicted escrow holder [to] shield himself or herself from liability, and protect the interests of the parties to the escrow as well. Interpleader is a safe harbor for the conflicted stakeholder. An escrow holder who fails to implead acts at his or her own peril." *Id.* To qualify for an interpleader action, a party must be one against whom multiple persons may make claims that "give rise to double or multiple liability." Columbia Code of Civil Procedure § 386. In such a case, the party "may bring an action against the claimants to compel them to interplead and litigate their several claims." Id. In other words, an interpleader action allows the party with current possession of the property bring all claimants to the property into court to settle who has true ownership.

If the court finds that the party is qualified to bring an interpleader action, "an interlocutory decree is entered which requires the defendants to interplead and litigate their claims to the funds. Upon deposit of monies with the court, the plaintiff then may be discharged from liability and dismissed from the interpleader action." *Diaz*

In *Diaz*, the escrow holder was a bank that was set to close a deal for the purchase of a restaurant. The bank had a validly executed agreement that had escrow instructions listing the price of the sale as $7,000. Both of the parties had signed this document. Later, one of the parties notified the court that the $7,000 figure was actually in error; the agreement was actually supposed to be for $19,000. Nevertheless, the Bank decided to close the deal for $7,000, in part because neither of the parties had sought an interpleader action. But the court said there is no authority for an escrow holder to close a contested deal instead of holding the property or interpleading it.

Here, Conner should qualify under the interpleader statute. That statute—as stated above—basically requires that the party seeking an interpleader action be one against whom multiple parties may make a claim. Certainly, Virta has already made a claim for recovery of his certificates. But it is also likely that B-G Investors may seek to compel Conner to deliver the certificates to the Trust Company. Conner has stated that they adamantly want the deal to close. They may try to force him—as their agent—to close the deal and deliver the stocks to the Trust Company.

Thus, courts appear to prefer escrow holders in Conner's position to interplead the two parties. Though, as Conner said, he would rather not have to sue his own clients. Nevertheless, it would quickly absolve Conner and the firm of any liability.

3. Do nothing immediately and retain possession of the stock certificates, until seller sues or parties work out a settlement.

As stated by the *Diaz* court, keeping disputed property in escrow benefits both parties because they "tend to be predisposed to resolution." In fact, the Diaz court held that a "reasonable construction of the escrow instructions required the Bank, upon receipt of the [letter disputing the sale price], to at least hold up closure until the situation was clarified." *Id.*

Here, there is a similar situation—both parties dispute whether the conditions have been met to close the deal. At very least, as escrow holder, Conner has a duty to clarify the situation before closing the deal. He has attempted to do this, and remained hopeful that the deal would close. He urged the other side to work positively to come to a settlement. He even suggested that they should calculate the additional tax burden of the amended payment schedule and make a counteroffer, adding it to the selling price.

But it has become clear that Virta has no interest in settling. His lawyer Taylor responded that the deal had been revoked and demanded return of the shares. Thus, it doesn't appear likely that our holding on to the shares will lead to any sort of positive, mutual settlement. Virta wants to walk away. Nor does it seem particularly wise to force Virta to sue. As Virta's escrow holder, Conner has a duty to follow his instructions. It is clear he will not settle, and the courts do not seem to like it when an escrow holder forces one of his principals into the situation where he has to sue.

Thus, because there is no likelihood of settlement, and because putting a principal in the position of having to sue is disliked by the courts and may precipitate a bad judgment against Conner and the firm, it is unadvisable to hold on to the shares.

Conclusion

Because Conner has become an escrow holder with fiduciary duties to Virta, his potential liabilities—and the potential liabilities of the firm—could be astronomical. He certainly should not close the deal, which could trigger contract and tort actions—including the possibility of punitive damages. Nor is it advisable that he hold on to the certificates in an attempt to foster a settlement. Virta is not interested in settling.

The last option for the firm—and mostly likely also for Conner himself—is to bring an interpleader action. Even though this would mean suing our own clients, it would absolve the firm of all liability. Thus, it is the preferred option.

PT-A: SELECTED ANSWER 2

PART I

A. Did Conner become an escrow holder for all the parties?

Most likely a court would find that yes, Conner did become an escrow holder for all the parties. Columbia Professional Code Section 17003 states that "escrow" means "any transaction in which one person, for the purpose of effecting the sale [of] ... personal property to another person, delivers any written instrument, money, evidence of title to real or personal property, or other thing of value to a third person to be held by that third person until the happening of a specified event or the performance of a prescribed condition, when it is then to be delivered by that third person to a grantee, grantor, promisee, promisor, obligee, obligor, bailee, bailor, or any agent or employee of any of the latter."

Here, the facts of our situation fit into the Professional Code's definition of escrow quite neatly. In Conner's case, Virta ("one person") gave him (the "third party") the share certificates ("evidence of title to personal property" or "other thing of value") on February 17th, to be held until the deal closes (the "happening of a specified event"). More specifically, the deal would not close until after the purchase agreement and promissory note were signed and after Virta acknowledged receipt of a down payment of $500,000. After the deal closed, Conner was to give the share certificates to BTI's transfer agent. Under these facts, it seems that Conner is clearly an escrow agent.

To bolster this point, the case law supports the idea that an attorney in Conner's situation would be seen by courts to be acting as an escrow agent. In Wasman v. Seiden, attorney Hartman (on behalf of his client, Kenneth) gave attorney Seiden (acting on behalf of his client, Barbara) a grant deed conveying a piece of real property to Seiden's client, but was explicitly told that Seiden did not have authorization to record the grant deed until Kenneth received $70,000 in cash or promissory note from Barbara. In this case, Seiden was found by the court to be acting as an escrow agent. Paraphrasing the Professional Code section 17003, the court reasoned: "An escrow is created when, for the purpose of facilitating a transaction, property is delivered to an escrow holder to be held until the conditions specified in agreed-upon instructions are fulfilled, when the property is to be delivered to another according to the instructions." The court further went on to state that explicit acceptance of the duty of care of an escrow agent is not necessary, and that the court is permitted to infer that mere acceptance of the grant deed is enough to compel the attorney to follow the instructions given. The court seems to imply that this inference is allowable particularly in cases when the facts show that property is being given to the escrow agent as a good faith attempt to facilitate settlement.

This case is directly analogous to the situation Conner finds himself in now. Like Seiden, he willingly accepted property/documents to facilitate a transaction, and was given clear instructions as to when that property should be released. Moreover, Virta gave the share certificates to Conner in what appears to be a good faith attempt to close the deal. It is therefore very likely that a court would not only hold Conner to be acting as an escrow agent, but that as an escrow agent Conner was bound by the specific instructions he was given regarding the conditions that would allow him to transfer the share certificates.

B. If Conner acted as an escrow holder, was it proper for him to be an attorney for one party and an escrow holder for all parties?

Most likely a court would find that Conner could properly act as both an attorney for one party and an escrow holder for all parties.

In fact, Conner is only allowed to act as the parties' escrow agent because he is representing one of the parties. Section 17002 of the Columbia Professional Code specifies that it is permissible for a person to act as an escrow agent when "Licensed to practice law in Columbia who has a bona fide client relationship with a principal in a real estate or personal property transaction and who is not actively engaged in the business of an escrow agent."

Under this law, B-T and Conner have a bona fide client relationship, B-T is a principal in the personal property transaction, being the buyer, and Conner is not actively engaged in the business of an escrow agent. There is nothing wrong with Conner having taken on the role of the escrow agent in this situation. To further bolster this point, the court opinion in Wasman is once again instructional. In that case, the court concluded by reiterating that attorneys are in fact encouraged to act as escrow agents. "[I]t is both useful and commonplace to entrust attorneys with closing documents, settlement agreements, releases, funds, and other items."

C. If Conner acted in this dual capacity, does it restrict his ability both to advise his clients and to follow their instructions?

This is a complicated question, but based on the case law Conner is only restricted in one sense: he cannot follow their instructions if it interferes with his duty as a bailee to "keep property and not dispose of it without the authority of the depositor" (Wasman). Conner's duties to his own clients remain, and he has unrestricted ability to advise them, but he cannot follow their instructions if it would lead to him releasing the share certificates without Virta's authorization. To be more precise, Conner cannot follow his clients' instruction if it would lead him to close escrow against the instructions agreed upon by both parties.

D. If Conner is an escrow holder, what are his duties to the opposing party?

Normally, courts have found that attorneys have no duty to adverse parties (Wasman). However, when the attorney has taken on the role of an escrow agent, as Conner likely has here, a new duty is imposed. Conner now has a fiduciary duty to Virta, and is obligated to comply strictly to the escrow instructions. In this case, this means Connor has the duty to protect Virta's share certificates until the deal has closed, which would not happen until the purchase agreement and promissory note were signed and Virta had acknowledged receipt of a $500,000 deposit to his account. At that point, Conner would be authorized to transfer the share certificates to B-T.

Part II

Options:

1. Complete the purchase and forward stock certificates for transfer

This is likely the most dangerous option for our firm to take. There are two causes of action that Virta may raise against our firm if we complete the purchase.

First, Virta may raise a tort claim of conversion. As laid out in <u>Wasman</u>, the elements of a conversion claim are: 1) the plaintiff's ownership or right to possession of the property; 2) the defendant's conversion by a wrongful act or disposition of property rights; and 3) damages. Here, Virta had ownership of the share certificates, and if Conner transfers them to B-T, he will have converted them, potentially leading to damages for Virta. The only question here is whether the conversion is by a "wrongful act or disposition." In <u>Wasman</u>, the court found that if the escrow agent transferred the property he was obliged to protect without the express authorization of the depositor, then the transfer would be considered wrongful.

Here, a court is likely to find that Conner's transfer is wrongful, because the facts show that the required conditions for the escrow have not been met. Namely, the deal has not closed yet. In order for the deal to close, the promissory note and purchase agreement must be signed, and Virta has to have acknowledged receipt of a deposit of $500,000. These things must happen *before* Conner is properly allowed to transfer the share certificates. However, there are two problems: First, the facts show that Virta has not yet acknowledged receipt of the deposit; and second, Virta revoked his offer to sell his shares before B-T had a chance to sign the purchase agreement or promissory note. As to the first problem, although the facts show that B-T deposited the required cash into Virta's account, the explicit terms of the escrow agreement stated that it was Virta's acknowledgement that was necessary, not B-T's. As to the second issue, contract law states that an offer (here, the purchase agreement) is revocable at any point before mutual assent is established. This transaction falls under the statute of frauds due to involving over $500 worth of property, and therefore mutual assent can only be established by signing the agreement.

One may be tempted to raise a defense that Conner did not intentionally, wrongfully convert the shares. The fact that B-T assured Conner that Virta still wanted to close shows Conner had reason to believe Virta was merely negotiating, and the fact that B-T deposited $500,000 into Virta's account shows that there was a good faith effort not to commit the tort of conversion. However, Wasman has established that the escrow agent's state of mind is irrelevant. "Good or bad faith, care or negligence, and knowledge or ignorance, are ordinarily immaterial ... The misdelivery of entrusted property of another constitutes a conversion of it even though he acted innocently and by mistake." Conner would therefore still be liable for the tort of conversion even though he had no bad intention.

Second, Virta may raise a claim for breach of Conner's duty to strictly follow agreed-upon instructions (or a breach of contract claim), as raised in the case Diaz v United Columbia Bank. In that case, the bank was acting as an escrow agent between two parties. Two main issues were raised in that case: 1) whether, when two parties had agreed to the escrow instructions, one party could unilaterally change the instructions; and 2) whether an escrow agent may still close after being given notice of a possible error in the escrow instructions.

As to the first issue, the court found that no one party was allowed to unilaterally change the instructions. A court might argue that Conner's alteration of the promissory note could be construed as altering the instructions, because Virta implicitly agreed only to the terms of the original promissory note. A court would have to face the question of if the replacement promissory note was valid. While technically Virta was only required to sign the purchase agreement (which remained unchanged on its face), the purchase agreement was implicitly changed because the promissory note referenced within it was replaced by a new one, with new terms. Depending on the case law, a court might find either way.

As to the second issue, a court is likely to find that Conner was given notice of competing demands regarding a material fact. While there did not appear to be an error on the face of the instructions given, Conner had been given plenty of evidence that a conflict in the desires of the parties had arisen. Through Conner's communications with B-T, and the revocation letter from Virta, a court is likely to see that Conner was well aware of this conflict. In fact, by amending the promissory note Conner has impliedly admitted that he knew of the conflict, but instead of taking proper action to other authorities, attempted to unilaterally address the conflict himself on behalf of his client. There are three major points of contention: 1) the schedule for payments, 2) the deadline for closing, and 3) whether Virta validly revoked the agreement before closing. Although, as Conner notes in his interview, the schedule for payments and the deadline are both arguably minor, and therefore may not be not material facts, he would be hard-pressed to argue that the revocation of the agreement is immaterial.

In Diaz the court explicitly states that in the face of competing desires regarding a material term of the instructions, an escrow agent must either hold the property or interplead it in order to satisfy the requirement to exercise reasonable skill and ordinary diligence.

Moreover, by going ahead and closing, Conner may end up facing punitive damages under Civil Code section 3294. Under that code, punitive damages may be awarded when there is clear and convincing evidence that the defendant acted with "conscious and deliberate disregard of the interests of others that his conduct may be called willful or wanton." The court then concluded that this requirement was met when an escrow agent closes, "knowing full well that there is a dispute as to the terms of the escrow." Here, the facts show that Conner had many reasons to know that there was a dispute ongoing between Virta and B-T. Even if we discount the second-hand information Conner received from B-T, the moment he received a notice of revocation from Virta he was put on notice that there was a dispute, and closing should no longer have been an option until the dispute was settled.

As a final note, Conner has cited Commercial Code section 8403 as a potential remedy for Virta if we went ahead and closed. Conner is technically correct; however, this is an unwise move, as it forces Virta to go to court to seek relief (injunctive or otherwise). The code section does not provide direct relief; it only allows Virta to demand the issuer of the shares to withhold registration of the transfer for 30 days until he can seek legal process. As analyzed above, the last thing we want is to push Virta into litigation where Conner may be held liable as an escrow agent.

To conclude, completing the purchase is by far our worst option, and is likely to lead to us being liable for the tort of conversion, a breach of contract, and punitive damages. Although Conner might find it slightly embarrassing to have to backpedal that way, his temporary discomfort and the minor hit to our professional reputation is likely nothing compared to the damages we may have to pay if Conner is liable for the above claims.

2. File an interpleader action against our clients and the seller

This is likely our firm's best option, as it provides a safe harbor that would remove the firm from any escrow agent liability.

As laid out in Diaz, interpleader would save Conner from all of the liabilities which he might otherwise face, as discussed above. According to Diaz, "By implementing an interpleader action and obtaining a discharge from further liability the stakeholder avoids tort liability." In this way, Conner can effectively wash his hands of the duties of an escrow agent, and return to representing B-T alone, with no duties owed to Virta. Once the court takes charge, they can then focus on the issues of whether the escrow agreement was breached by Virta when he attempted to revoke the agreement, and/or by B-T when they amended the promissory note and signed the purchase agreement after Virta's attempted revocation.

Regardless of the outcome of that case, our firm will not be liable for any breach due to Conner's role as an escrow agent.

3. Do nothing immediately and retain possession of the stock certificates, until seller sues or parties work out a settlement

While this option is certainly better than completing the purchase, it still pales in comparison to the option of interpleading. According to Diaz, when an escrow agent has notice of a dispute between the parties, he has a duty to exercise reasonable skill and ordinary diligence. The court explicitly goes on to state that a reasonable response would be either to hold the property until the dispute is resolved, or to interplead it. The court appears to favor interpleader, but either route is acceptable.

However, if we should choose to hold the property, Conner remains liable as an escrow agent. This leaves the firm vulnerable, as it would allow either party to seek out tort recovery if the negotiations turn south.

Essentially, this option is only the most favorable if we determine that the parties are very likely to be able to negotiate a deal. As reasoned in Diaz "Once escrow has been closed in such a manner as to make one party feel victimized and to force that party to hire a litigator to assert his or her rights, the changes of a speedy resolution diminish." Although the court was referring to closing the escrow account, the same idea holds true for interpleader. By forcing the parties to go to court to resolve their dispute, we would potentially be forcing them into a more adverse relationship than is necessary.

In this case, assuming Virta has not been too angered by this whole proceeding, it does seem likely that this might be the best option. Virta and B-T are only disputing a small change (the scheduling of payments), not something that should cause a large amount of harm to either party. Moreover, Virta's problem with the deadline appears to be largely because he was not convinced B-T would be paying him at all. Since B-T has already paid the deposit, it seems likely that Virta might let the deadline issue go.

All that said, Virta does seem angry and may no longer be willing to work with us at all. This being the case, we may want to consider interpleader instead, as it provides us better protection from liability arising from Conner's role as the escrow agent. My recommendation is to set up a final meeting with Virta and his attorney to assess the possibility of continuing negotiations. If Virta appears adamant that the sale is off, then we should seek out interpleader.

February 2015

California
Bar
Examination

Performance Test B
INSTRUCTIONS AND FILE

STATE v. DANIEL

STATE v. DANIEL

INSTRUCTIONS

1. This performance test is designed to evaluate your ability to handle a select number of legal authorities in the context of a factual problem involving a client.

2. The problem is set in the fictional State of Columbia, one of the United States.

3. You will have two sets of materials with which to work: a File and a Library.

4. The File contains factual materials about your case. The first document is a memorandum containing the instructions for the tasks you are to complete.

5. The Library contains the legal authorities needed to complete the tasks. The case reports may be real, modified, or written solely for the purpose of this performance test. If the cases appear familiar to you, do not assume that they are precisely the same as you have read before. Read each thoroughly, as if it were new to you. You should assume that cases were decided in the jurisdictions and on the dates shown. In citing cases from the Library, you may use abbreviations and omit page citations.

6. You should concentrate on the materials provided, but you should also bring to bear on the problem your general knowledge of the law. What you have learned in law school and elsewhere provides the general background for analyzing the problem; the File and Library provide the specific materials with which you must work.

7. Although there are no restrictions on how you apportion your time, you should probably allocate at least 90 minutes to reading and organizing before you begin preparing your response.

8. Your response will be graded on its compliance with instructions and on its content, thoroughness, and organization.

LYNCH and MAURER

Attorneys at Law

Avery Park, Columbia

MEMORANDUM

TO:	Applicant
FROM:	Mary Lynch
RE:	State v. Daniel
DATE:	February 26, 2015

We represent Christopher Daniel, who has been charged with the murder of Peter Daniel and the attempted murder of Gloria Daniel. Christopher is their son. Unfortunately, Gloria Daniel has recently died and I expect the indictment to be amended to charge Christopher with her murder as well.

I have filed a notice of a motion seeking to suppress evidence. We have ten days after filing this notice to file the supporting memorandum of points and authorities. Please prepare a draft of a persuasive memorandum of points and authorities that argues that the motion should be granted in full or at least in part. You may assume that, at the evidentiary hearing, witnesses will testify consistent with the material contained in the file. The transcript contained in the file is a certified copy of the recording. As such, you may assume that, if any parts of the recording are admitted into evidence, the transcript of that portion will also be admitted.

Arguments on motions to suppress require a detailed showing of how the facts in the case relate to specific factors identified by the courts in suppression cases. Therefore, your memorandum should relate specific facts to those specific factors and conclude how your analysis would establish that the evidence should be suppressed. Take care to anticipate arguments the prosecution is likely to make and explain why they are not persuasive. Your memorandum should, of course, contain appropriate argument headings, but should dispense with a statement of facts. I will draft the statement of facts later.

STATE OF COLUMBIA

WARREN COUNTY SUPERIOR COURT

STATE OF COLUMBIA	Criminal Division
v.	CASE NO. 2014-2341
CHRISTOPHER DANIEL	

NOTICE OF MOTION TO SUPPRESS EVIDENCE

PLEASE TAKE NOTICE that, upon the attached affidavit of Dr. Nancy Donahue, and upon all the previous papers and proceedings in this matter, the undersigned will move this Court at the Courthouse located at 1435 Elm Street, Avery Park, Columbia, on March 5, 2015 at 9:00 a.m., or as soon thereafter as counsel can be heard, for an order:

1. Suppressing evidence of all or part of all testimony of nonverbal statements allegedly made by Gloria Daniel to the police during an interview conducted on August 12-13, 2014, as inadmissible hearsay, or in the alternative, a violation of defendant's constitutional right to confront witnesses, and

2. Suppressing evidence of all or part of all transcripts or testimony recording concerning the 911 call allegedly made by Peter Daniel on August 12-13, 2014, as inadmissible hearsay and a violation of defendant's constitutional right to confront witnesses, and

3. For such other and further relief as the Court may deem just and proper.

DATED: February 25, 2015

___/s/ Mary Lynch_____

Mary Lynch
Attorney for Defendant

STATE OF COLUMBIA

WARREN COUNTY SUPERIOR COURT

STATE OF COLUMBIA	Criminal Division
v.	CASE NO. 2014-2341
CHRISTOPHER DANIEL	

AFFIDAVIT OF DR. NANCY DONAHUE
IN SUPPORT OF DEFENDANT'S MOTION TO SUPPRESS EVIDENCE

I, Dr. Nancy Donahue, being duly sworn, state:

1. I am a medical doctor and board certified neurologist licensed to practice in the state of Columbia.

2. I have expertise in neurology and rehabilitation of people with brain injuries.

3. I am one of Gloria Daniel's treating physicians.

4. I am Department Chair of Neurology at Avery Park Health Systems.

5. I started treating Mrs. Daniel in October 2014.

6. I have reviewed the statements of police and first responders who assisted Mrs. Daniel on August 13, 2014, as well as her entire medical record.

7. Many people with brain injuries have erratic movements of their arms and legs.

8. In order to know if someone who moved her head up and down or side to side was actually answering a question, I would have to know much more about her mental status than is contained in medical records or witness accounts to determine if the movement was actually in response to the question, and/or if it was accurate.

9. There are brain injury patients who may nod their heads up and down, but do not really intend the "yes" response.

10. In order to assess such a person's movements and responses, I would first have to ask a series of questions in order to establish if the person was oriented to person, place, or time. Next, to determine if the individual was competent to answer

questions, I would ask simple and unambiguous questions to which the answer was immediately apparent, e.g., "Are you a woman?"

11. Even if a brain-injured person was oriented and able to follow commands, those facts did not mean the person had any memory of the event that caused the brain injury.

12. When police come to my facility to question someone with a brain injury, I first assess the person to determine if he or she can provide any useful information.

13. If the person is not oriented, even if he or she can follow simple commands, no useful information can be provided.

14. Even if Mrs. Daniel was oriented and could generally answer questions, it was very unlikely that she would have any memory of the event that caused the injury.

15. With such a serious brain injury, it was extremely unlikely, if not impossible, that Mrs. Daniel could have remembered the event that caused the injury.

___/s/ Nancy Donahue_____
Nancy Donahue, M.D.

Subscribed and sworn to before me on February 25, 2015   [Signature and Title]

PRELIMINARY HEARING TESTIMONY OF TYLER JAMES

BY: MELISSA BREGER, Deputy District Attorney

* * * * *

BREGER: I have a few questions.

JAMES: Fine.

BREGER: Officer James, can you tell us where you were on the evening of August 12-13, 2014?

JAMES: I was on patrol in the Newtown section of the city.

BREGER: That is here in Avery Park?

JAMES: Yes.

BREGER: Did you respond to a call?

JAMES: Yes.

BREGER: What was the nature of the call?

JAMES: The 911 operator said that there was an assault taking place at 365 Delmar Street and I immediately went there.

BREGER: Approximately what time was this?

JAMES: About 12:30 a.m.; so I guess it was the 13th.

BREGER: When you got there, who did you see when you first went into the residence?

JAMES: When I first went into the room, there was one person in the front room. He was a man later identified as Peter Daniel. And then there was a woman lying in front of the refrigerator in the kitchen who was identified as Gloria Daniel.

BREGER: All right. When you first went in there, in what kind of condition was Mr. Daniel?

JAMES:	He was dead. He had a wound to the head that we later learned was caused by a baseball bat. He was lying in blood. It looked like he fell over when he died. In fact, he had a telephone in his hand. He apparently pulled the phone cord out of the wall when he fell.
BREGER:	And did you approach Mr. Daniel?
JAMES:	Yes, I did, but it was clear he was dead.
BREGER:	What did you do then?
JAMES:	I went into the kitchen, and saw Mrs. Daniel.
BREGER:	What condition was she in?
JAMES:	She also appeared to have a head wound. She was also severely beaten around her face.
BREGER:	What did you do?
JAMES:	I got on my handheld radio and made sure the emergency medical team was on its way. After that, I went back to Mrs. Daniel.
BREGER:	Did you speak to her?
JAMES:	Yes, I reassured her that help was on the way and asked her if there was anyone else in the house.
BREGER:	Did she say anything?
JAMES:	No, it was pretty clear she had suffered some kind of head injury and she was unable to speak.
BREGER:	What happened then?
JAMES:	I went to search the house to make sure the assailant was not still present.
BREGER:	Was there anyone else in the house?
JAMES:	Just Mr. Daniel.
BREGER:	Then what happened?
JAMES:	I went back to Mrs. Daniel.
BREGER:	From the time you went to clear the house and the time you returned to Mrs. Daniel, how long was that?

JAMES: It was probably 10 minutes. It was a big house. Sometime during the search I heard that the ambulance had arrived, so I knew she was being attended to.

BREGER: When you went back to Mrs. Daniel, what happened?

JAMES: She was already on the gurney to be taken to the hospital, but I stopped them and I asked if I could have a few moments with her. So, the paramedics stopped.

BREGER: Then what happened?

JAMES: I asked her if she knew who had done this to her and her husband. She tried to speak, but again, couldn't.

BREGER: Then what happened?

JAMES: Based on what the 911 operator told me, I asked her whether a member of her family did this and she nodded yes. Then I asked whether her son Jonathan did this. She shook her head no. Then I asked whether her son Christopher had done this. She nodded yes.

BREGER: Then what did you do?

JAMES: I repeated the question about Christopher two more times and she nodded, yes, both times. Then the paramedics put her in the ambulance.

* * * * *

STATEMENT OF KEVIN ROBERT

I am a paramedic employed by the Avery Park Fire Department. I was a first responder to the scene of the Daniel murder and assault, 365 Delmar Street, on August 12-13, 2014. When my partner, Leonard Ickes, and I arrived at the Daniel residence we found Peter Daniel dead in the living room and Gloria Daniel on the kitchen floor. She had profound injuries.

Mrs. Daniel was obviously in extreme distress. She was agitated and frustrated that she was unable to speak and her legs were moving erratically back and forth. I attempted to give Mrs. Daniel oxygen and assess her injuries. I realized she would need to be intubated, so I radioed for medical permission to give her a sedative necessary for the intubation. I inserted an IV line to administer the sedative. I administered the sedative. She responded to the sedative and calmed down.

As I was moving her to the ambulance, Officer Tyler James stopped Leonard and me and asked to speak to Mrs. Daniel. I explained that she was unable to speak, but Officer James asked her if her son Christopher had done this to her. She nodded yes. He asked her the same question a second time and she again nodded yes.

___/s/ Kevin Robert_____
Kevin Robert

LYNCH and MAURER

Attorneys at Law

Avery Park, Columbia

MEMORANDUM

TO: State v. Daniel File

FROM: Mary Lynch

RE: Summary of Interview of Gloria Daniel

DATE: February 11, 2015

---

1.   She is the mother of the defendant in the above-entitled action.

2.   I spoke with her at the Avery Park Hospital.

3.   She remains in serious condition and the prognosis for her recovering is not good.

4.   At approximately 12:10 a.m. on August 13, 2014, she was attacked by an unknown assailant in her house on Delmar Street, Avery Park, Columbia.

5.   I informed her that Officer Tyler James allegedly attempted to question her in her home on August 13, 2014.

6.   I explained that Officer James allegedly asked her if she recognized the assailant who attacked her and killed her husband, Peter Daniel.

7.   She indicated that at the time of the questioning by Officer James she was in deep pain and suffering from a head injury, making it impossible to speak and, therefore, could not have responded to any questions.

8.   She has no recollection of being questioned by Officer James on August 13, 2014.

9.   She was unable to speak for over one month following the attack on her and murder of her husband.

10. She claims that at no time has she identified who the attacker was.

11. She does not know who attacked her and killed her husband the evening of August 12-13, 2014.

LYNCH and MAURER

Attorneys at Law

Avery Park, Columbia

MEMORANDUM

TO: State v. Daniel File

FROM: Mary Lynch

RE: Summary of Interview of Harry Robinson

DATE: February 11, 2015

I spoke with Chief Robinson of the state police today by telephone. He indicated the following:

1. He went to Christopher Daniel's dorm room in College Station and questioned him at approximately 8:30 a.m. on August 13, 2014.

2. Christopher indicated that he was a student at Columbia State University in College Park.

3. Christopher indicated that he had been in his dorm room all night.

4. Christopher said he did not remember seeing anyone who could confirm his presence in the dorm.

5. Robinson asked to see Christopher's car.

6. Christopher identified a yellow Taurus, license plate 274 SUR, as his car.

7. It takes approximately 2½ to 3 hours to drive from College Station to Avery Park.

911 Call Made August 13, 2014
12:43 a.m.

911:	911, what is your emergency?
CALLER:	(background noise – heavy breathing)
911:	Hello, 911. What is your emergency?
CALLER:	Hello.
911:	Hello, this is Avery Park Police. Are you trying to call 911?
CALLER:	Uh, I've been beaten. It was a bat. My wife too.
911:	What's going on?
CALLER:	He left. He just drove off.
911:	What's that?
CALLER:	He just, he just left me.
911:	Who just left you?
CALLER:	My son. He's probably heading back to college.
911:	So, what's going on there?
CALLER:	My son. He's killed his mother.
911:	I am sending police officers and an ambulance now. Hold on. Stay on the line.
CALLER:	He's driving a Ford Taurus.
911:	Sir, please hold on. Help is on the way. Sir, what is your son's name?
CALLER:	Jonathan and Christopher.
911:	Who did this?
CALLER:	(unintelligible) . . . .
911:	Sir, what color is the Taurus?
CALLER:	Yellow.
911:	Sir, do you know the license plate number?
CALLER:	The license plate is 274 . . . .
911:	Sir, are you at 365 Delmar Street?
CALLER:	. . . . SUR.

911:	Sir, where are you?
CALLER:	In the house; the living room.
911:	Okay, sir. Tell me where your wife is.
CALLER:	274 SUR . . . .
911:	274?
CALLER:	(unintelligible)
911:	Sir, what is your son's name?
CALLER:	(unintelligible)
911:	Sir?
CALLER:	He was supposed to be (unintelligible) . . . .
911:	Sir? Sir? Are you there Mr. Daniel?

Call Disconnected.

February 2015

California
Bar
Examination

Performance Test B
LIBRARY

STATE v. DANIEL

LIBRARY

SELECTED PROVISIONS
COLUMBIA RULES OF EVIDENCE

Rule 104. Preliminary Questions

(a)   Questions of admissibility generally.—Preliminary questions concerning the qualification of a person to be a witness, the existence of a privilege, or the admissibility of evidence shall be determined by the court, subject to the provisions of subdivision (b). In making its determination it is not bound by the rules of evidence except those with respect to privileges.

(b) Relevancy conditioned on fact.—When the relevancy of evidence depends upon the fulfillment of a condition of fact, the court shall admit it upon, or subject to, the introduction of evidence sufficient to support a finding of the fulfillment of the condition.

* * *

Rule 401. Definition of "Relevant Evidence"

"Relevant evidence" means evidence having any tendency to make the existence of any fact that is of consequence to the determination of the action more or less probable than it would be without the evidence.

* * *

Rule 801. Definitions

The following definitions apply under this article:

(a)   Statement.—A "statement" is (1) an oral or written assertion or (2) nonverbal conduct of a person, if it is intended by the person as an assertion.

(b) Declarant.—A "declarant" is a person who makes a statement.

(c)   Hearsay.—"Hearsay" is a statement, other than one made by the declarant while testifying at the trial or hearing, offered in evidence to prove the truth of the matter asserted.

* * *

Rule 803. Hearsay Exceptions; Availability of Declarant Immaterial

The following are not excluded by the hearsay rule, even though the declarant is available as a witness:

* * *

(2) Excited utterance.—A statement relating to a startling event or condition made while the declarant was under the stress of excitement caused by the event or condition.

* * *

(8) Public records and reports.—Records, reports, statements, or data compilations, in any form, of public offices or agencies, setting forth (A) the activities of the office or agency, or (B) matters observed pursuant to duty imposed by law as to which matters there was a duty to report, excluding, however, in criminal cases matters observed by police officers and other law enforcement personnel, or (C) in civil actions and proceedings and against the Government in criminal cases, factual findings resulting from an investigation made pursuant to authority granted by law, unless the sources of information or other circumstances indicate lack of trustworthiness.

* * *

Rule 902. Self-Authentication

Extrinsic evidence of authenticity as a condition precedent to admissibility is not required with respect to the following:

* * *

(4) Certified copies of public records.—A copy of an official record or report or entry therein, or of a document authorized by law to be recorded or filed and actually recorded or filed in a public office, including data compilations in any form, certified as correct by the custodian or other person authorized to make the certification.

Crawford v. Washington

U.S. Supreme Court (2004)

Petitioner Michael Crawford stabbed a man who allegedly tried to rape his wife, Sylvia. At his trial, the State played for the jury Sylvia's tape-recorded statement to the police, made several hours after the stabbing, describing the stabbing. The Washington Supreme Court upheld petitioner's conviction after determining that Sylvia's statement was reliable. The question presented is whether this procedure complied with the Sixth Amendment's guarantee that, "[i]n all criminal prosecutions, the accused shall enjoy the right ... to be confronted with the witnesses against him."

The State charged petitioner with assault and attempted murder. At trial, he claimed self-defense. Sylvia did not testify because of the state marital privilege, which generally bars a spouse from testifying without the other spouse's consent. In Washington, this privilege does not extend to a spouse's out-of-court statements admissible under a hearsay exception, so the State sought to introduce Sylvia's tape-recorded statements to the police as evidence that the stabbing was not in self-defense. Noting that Sylvia had admitted she led petitioner to the victim's apartment and thus had facilitated the assault, the State invoked the hearsay exception for statements against penal interest.

We granted certiorari to determine whether the State's use of Sylvia's statement violated the Confrontation Clause.

History supports two inferences about the meaning of the Sixth Amendment.

First, the principal evil at which the Confrontation Clause was directed was the civil law mode of criminal procedure, and particularly its use of *ex parte* examinations as evidence against the accused. The Sixth Amendment must be interpreted with this focus in mind.

The text of the Confrontation Clause reflects this focus. It applies to "witnesses" against the accused -- in other words, those who "bear testimony." Testimony, in turn, is typically a solemn declaration or affirmation made for the purpose of establishing or proving some fact. An accuser who makes a formal statement to government officers bears testimony in a sense that a person who makes a casual remark to an acquaintance does not. The constitutional text, like the history underlying the common law right of confrontation, thus reflects an especially acute concern with a specific type of out-of-court statement.

Various formulations of this core class of "testimonial" statements exist: *ex parte* in-court testimony or its functional equivalent -- that is, material such as affidavits, custodial examinations, prior testimony that the defendant was unable to cross-examine, or similar pretrial statements that declarants would reasonably expect to be used prosecutorially; extrajudicial statements contained in formalized testimonial materials, such as affidavits, depositions, prior testimony, or confessions; statements that were made under circumstances that would lead an objective witness reasonably to believe that the statement would be available for use at a later trial. These formulations all share a common nucleus and then define the Clause's coverage at various levels of abstraction around it. Regardless of the precise articulation, some statements qualify under any definition -- for example, *ex parte* testimony at a preliminary hearing.

Statements taken by police officers in the course of interrogations are also testimonial under even a narrow standard. The statements are not sworn testimony, but the absence of oath was not dispositive.

That interrogators are police officers rather than magistrates does not change the picture either. Justices of the peace conducting examinations under civil law statutes were not magistrates as we understand that office today, but had an essentially investigative and prosecutorial function. The involvement of government officers in the production of testimonial evidence presents the same risk, whether the officers are police or justices of the peace.

In sum, even if the Sixth Amendment is not solely concerned with testimonial hearsay, that is its primary object, and interrogations by law enforcement officers fall squarely within that class.

The historical record also supports a second proposition: that the Framers would not have allowed admission of testimonial statements of a witness who did not appear at trial unless he was unavailable to testify, and the defendant had had a prior opportunity for cross-examination. The text of the Sixth Amendment does not suggest any open-ended exceptions from the confrontation requirement to be developed by the courts. Rather, the "right ... to be confronted with the witnesses against him" is most naturally read as a reference to the right of confrontation at common law, admitting only those exceptions established at the time of the founding. The common law in 1791 conditioned admissibility of an absent witness's examination on unavailability and a prior opportunity to cross-examine. The Sixth Amendment therefore incorporates those limitations.

We do not read the historical sources to say that a prior opportunity to cross-examine was merely a sufficient, rather than a necessary, condition for admissibility of testimonial statements. They suggest that this requirement was dispositive, and not merely one of several ways to establish reliability.

Our case law has been largely consistent with these two principles. Our cases have remained faithful to the Framers' understanding: Testimonial statements of witnesses absent from trial have been admitted only where the declarant is unavailable, and only where the defendant has had a prior opportunity to cross-examine.

Finally, to reiterate, when the declarant appears for cross-examination at trial, the Confrontation Clause places no constraints at all on the use of his prior testimonial statements. It is therefore irrelevant that the reliability of some out-of-court statements cannot be replicated, even if the declarant testifies to the same matters in court. The Clause does not bar admission of a statement so long as the declarant is present at trial to defend or explain it.

Dispensing with confrontation because testimony is obviously reliable is akin to dispensing with jury trial because a defendant is obviously guilty. This is not what the Sixth Amendment prescribes.

Where nontestimonial hearsay is at issue, it is wholly consistent with the Framers' design to afford the states flexibility in their development of hearsay law. Where testimonial evidence is at issue, however, the Sixth Amendment demands what the common law required: unavailability and a prior opportunity for cross-examination. We leave for another day any effort to spell out a comprehensive definition of "testimonial." Whatever else the term covers, it applies at a minimum to prior testimony at a preliminary hearing, before a grand jury, or at a former trial; and to police interrogations. These are the modern practices with closest kinship to the abuses at which the Confrontation Clause was directed.

In this case, the State admitted Sylvia's testimonial statement against petitioner, despite the fact that he had no opportunity to cross-examine her. That alone is sufficient to make out a violation of the Sixth Amendment.

The judgment of the Washington Supreme Court is reversed, and the case is remanded for further proceedings not inconsistent with this opinion.

Davis v. Washington

U.S. Supreme Court (2006)

This case requires us to determine when statements made to law enforcement personnel during a 911 call or at a crime scene are "testimonial" and thus subject to the requirements of the Sixth Amendment's Confrontation Clause.

The relevant statements were made to a 911 emergency operator on February 1, 2001. When the operator answered the initial call, the connection terminated before anyone spoke. She reversed the call, and Michelle McCottry answered. In the ensuing conversation, the operator ascertained that McCottry was involved in a domestic disturbance with her former boyfriend Adrian Davis, the petitioner in this case:

911 Operator: Hello.

Complainant: Hello.

911 Operator: What's going on?

Complainant: He's here jumpin' on me again.

911 Operator: Okay. Listen to me carefully. Are you in a house or an apartment?

Complainant: I'm in a house.

911 Operator: Are there any weapons?

Complainant: No. He's usin' his fists.

911 Operator: Okay. Has he been drinking?

Complainant: No.

911 Operator: Okay, sweetie. I've got help started. Stay on the line with me, okay?

Complainant: I'm on the line.

911 Operator: Listen to me carefully. Do you know his last name?

Complainant: It's Davis.

911 Operator: Davis? Okay, what's his first name?

Complainant: Adrian.

911 Operator: What is it?

Complainant: Adrian.

911 Operator: Adrian?

Complainant: Yeah.

911 Operator: Okay. What's his middle initial?

Complainant: Martell. He's runnin' now.

As the conversation continued, the operator learned that Davis had "just run out the door" after hitting McCottry, and that he was leaving in a car with someone else. McCottry started talking, but the operator cut her off, saying, "Stop talking and answer my questions." She then gathered more information about Davis (including his birthday), and learned that Davis had told McCottry that his purpose in coming to the house was "to get his stuff," since McCottry was moving. McCottry described the context of the assault, after which the operator told her that the police were on their way. "They're gonna check the area for him first," the operator said, "and then they're gonna come talk to you."

The police arrived within four minutes of the 911 call and observed McCottry's shaken state, the "fresh injuries on her forearm and her face," and her "frantic efforts to gather her belongings and her children so that they could leave the residence."

The State charged Davis with felony violation of a domestic no-contact order. The State's only witnesses were the two police officers who responded to the 911 call. Both officers testified that McCottry exhibited injuries that appeared to be recent, but neither officer could testify as to the cause of the injuries. McCottry presumably could have testified as to whether Davis was her assailant, but she did not appear. Over Davis's objection, based on the Confrontation Clause of the Sixth Amendment, the trial court admitted the recording of her exchange with the 911 operator, and the jury convicted him.

In *Crawford v. Washington* (U.S. 2004), we held that the Confrontation Clause bars "admission of testimonial statements of a witness who did not appear at trial unless he was unavailable to testify, and the defendant had had a prior opportunity for cross-examination." A critical portion of this holding, and the portion central to resolution of this case now before us, is the phrase "testimonial statements." Only statements of this sort cause the declarant to be a "witness" within the meaning of the Confrontation Clause. It is the testimonial character of the statement that separates it from other hearsay that, while subject to traditional limitations upon hearsay evidence, is not subject to the Confrontation Clause.

Without attempting to produce an exhaustive classification of all conceivable statements, or even all conceivable statements in response to police interrogation as either testimonial or nontestimonial, it suffices to decide the present case to hold as follows: Statements are nontestimonial when made in the course of police interrogation under circumstances objectively indicating that the primary purpose of the interrogation is to enable police assistance to meet an ongoing emergency. They are testimonial when the circumstances objectively indicate that there is no such ongoing emergency, and that the primary purpose of the interrogation is to establish or prove past events potentially relevant to later criminal prosecution.

If 911 operators are not themselves law enforcement officers, they may at least be agents of law enforcement when they conduct interrogations of 911 callers. For purposes of this opinion (and without deciding the point), we consider their acts to be acts of the police.

The question before us, then, is whether, objectively considered, the interrogation that took place in the course of the 911 call produced testimonial statements.

The difference between the interrogation here and the one in _Crawford_ is apparent on the face of things. Here, McCottry was speaking about events as they were actually happening, rather than describing past events. Sylvia Crawford's interrogation, on the other hand, took place hours after the events she described had occurred. Moreover, any reasonable listener would recognize that McCottry (unlike Sylvia Crawford) was facing an ongoing emergency. Although one might call 911 to provide a narrative report of a crime absent any imminent danger, McCottry's call was plainly a call for help against bona fide physical threat. Third, the nature of what was asked and answered in this case, again viewed objectively, was such that the elicited statements were necessary to be able to resolve the present emergency, rather than simply to learn (as in _Crawford_) what had happened in the past. That is true even of the operator's effort to establish the identity of the assailant, so that the dispatched officers might know whether they would be encountering a violent felon. And finally, the difference in the level of formality between the two interviews is striking. Crawford was responding calmly, at the station house, to a series of questions, with the officer-interrogator taping and making notes of her answers; McCottry's frantic answers were provided over the phone, in an environment that was not tranquil, or even (as far as any reasonable 911 operator could make out) safe.

We conclude from all this that the circumstances of McCottry's interrogation objectively indicate its primary purpose was to enable police assistance to meet an ongoing emergency. She simply was not acting as a witness; she was not testifying. What she said was not a weaker substitute for live testimony at trial. No "witness" goes into court to proclaim an emergency and seek help.

This is not to say that a conversation which begins as an interrogation to determine the need for emergency assistance cannot evolve into testimonial statements, once that purpose has been achieved. In this case, for example, after the operator gained the information needed to address the exigency of the moment, the emergency appears to have ended (when Davis drove away from the premises). The operator then told McCottry to be quiet, and proceeded to pose a battery of questions. It could readily be maintained that, from that point on, McCottry's statements were testimonial, not unlike the structured police questioning that occurred in *Crawford.*

We affirm the judgment of the Supreme Court of Washington.

Melendez-Diaz v. Massachusetts

U.S. Supreme Court (2009)

The Massachusetts courts in this case admitted into evidence affidavits reporting the results of forensic analysis that showed that material seized by the police and connected to the defendant was cocaine. The question presented is whether those affidavits are "testimonial," rendering the affiants "witnesses" subject to the defendant's right of confrontation under the Sixth Amendment.

Melendez-Diaz was charged with distributing cocaine and with trafficking in cocaine in an amount between 14 and 28 grams. At trial, the prosecution placed into evidence the bags seized. It also submitted three "certificates of analysis" showing the results of the forensic analysis performed on the seized substances. The certificates reported the weight of the seized bags and stated that the bags "have been examined with the following results: The substance was found to contain: Cocaine." The certificates were sworn to before a notary public by analysts at the State Laboratory Institute of the Massachusetts Department of Public Health, as required under Massachusetts law.

Petitioner objected to the admission of the certificates, asserting that our Confrontation Clause required the analysts to testify in person. The objection was overruled, and the certificates were admitted pursuant to state law as prima facie evidence of the composition, quality, and the net weight of the narcotic analyzed.

The jury found Melendez-Diaz guilty.

There is little doubt that the documents at issue in this case fall within the core class of testimonial statements as described in *Crawford v. Washington* (U.S. 2004). Our description of that category mentions affidavits. The documents at issue here, while denominated by Massachusetts law "certificates," are quite plainly affidavits: declarations of facts written down and sworn to by the declarant before an officer authorized to administer oaths. The fact in question is that the substance found in the possession of Melendez-Diaz and his codefendants was, as the prosecution claimed, cocaine -- the precise testimony the analysts would be expected to provide if called at trial. The "certificates" are functionally identical to live, in-court testimony, doing precisely what a witness does on direct examination.

Here, moreover, not only were the affidavits made under circumstances which would lead an objective witness reasonably to believe that the statement would be available for use at a later trial, but under Massachusetts law the sole purpose of the affidavits was to provide "prima facie evidence of the composition, quality, and the net weight" of the analyzed substance. We can safely assume that the analysts were aware of the affidavits' evidentiary purpose, since that purpose -- as stated in the relevant state law provision -- was reprinted on the affidavits themselves.

In short, under our decision in _Crawford_ the analysts' affidavits were testimonial statements, and the analysts were "witnesses" for purposes of the Sixth Amendment. Absent a showing that the analysts were unavailable to testify at trial and that petitioner had a prior opportunity to cross-examine them, petitioner was entitled to be confronted with the analysts at trial.

Confrontation is designed to weed out not only the fraudulent analyst, but the incompetent one as well. Serious deficiencies have been found in the forensic evidence used in criminal trials. Like expert witnesses generally, an analyst's lack of proper training or deficiency in judgment may be disclosed in cross-examination.

Respondent argues that the analysts' affidavits are admissible without confrontation because they are "akin to the types of official and business records admissible at common law." But the affidavits do not qualify as traditional official or business records, and even if they did, their authors would be subject to confrontation nonetheless.

Documents kept in the regular course of business may ordinarily be admitted at trial despite their hearsay status. _See_ Fed. Rule Evid. 803(6). But that is not the case if the regularly conducted business activity is the production of evidence for use at trial.

Respondent also misunderstands the relationship between the business and official records hearsay exceptions and the Confrontation Clause. Most of the hearsay exceptions covered statements that by their nature were not testimonial--for example, business records or statements in furtherance of a conspiracy. Business and public records are generally admissible absent confrontation not because they qualify under an exception to the hearsay rules, but because, having been created for the administration of an entity's affairs and not for the purpose of establishing or proving some fact at trial, they are not testimonial. Whether or not they qualify as business or official records, the analysts' statements here -- prepared specifically for use at petitioner's trial -- were testimony against petitioner, and the analysts were subject to confrontation under the Sixth Amendment.

This case involves little more than the application of our holding in *Crawford v. Washington*. The Sixth Amendment does not permit the prosecution to prove its case via *ex parte* out-of-court affidavits, and the admission of such evidence against Melendez-Diaz was error. We therefore reverse the judgment of the Appeals Court of Massachusetts and remand the case for further proceedings not inconsistent with this opinion.

People v. Jackson

Supreme Court of Columbia (2009)

Defendant-Appellant Junior Salas Jackson appeals from a conviction on two charges of misdemeanor assault and one charge of misdemeanor family violence stemming from an auto-pedestrian collision involving his girlfriend, Julie Sandra Muna Gadia. Jackson asserts that the trial court erred in admitting out-of-court statements made by witness-victim Gadia as an excited utterance exception under Rule of Evidence 803(2) where such statements were made in response to police officers' questions nearly a week after being run over by a truck.

On the night of August 3, 2007, Emergency Medical Technicians (EMTs) and police officers found Gadia in critical condition after being run over by a 1997 Mazda pickup truck belonging to Gadia's boyfriend, Jackson. Gadia experienced such a degree of physical trauma that she could not verbally respond to the EMTs and all she could do was move her eyes in response to light and groan in pain. She was transferred to the Naval Hospital where she underwent surgery.

Gadia spent nearly a week recovering in the Intensive Care Unit of the Naval Hospital. On August 9, 2007, at around 11:55 a.m., Officer Donald Nakamura was informed that Gadia was awake and said that Jackson ran her over twice. Lt. Krejci of the Naval Hospital told Officer Nakamura that Gadia would be more awake and responsive for an interview in a few hours after the sedatives wore off.

At around 2:00 p.m. the same day, Officer Nakamura was informed that Gadia was more responsive. At 2:38 p.m., Officer Nakamura arrived at the Naval Hospital and met with Lt. Krejci, who said that Gadia spoke softly because the ventilator tube was recently removed from her mouth. Officer Nakamura then interviewed Gadia. After Gadia began coughing heavily and started to moan, Officer Nakamura ended the interview and informed Gadia that he would return at a later time to interview her again.

At the trial, Gadia testified that she did not remember speaking to Officer Nakamura on August 9, 2007.

The trial court admitted into evidence excerpts from Officer Nakamura's report which recorded what Gadia said during an interview on August 9, 2007. The trial court found that, since Jackson would have the opportunity to cross-examine the declarant and test the reliability of Officer Nakamura, Jackson's confrontation rights would be satisfied. On the stand, Officer Nakamura read aloud:

> I inquired from ... Gadia if it was an accident. [G]adia informed me in a low, slurred tone of voice, that he did it on purpose. I inquired from her to whom was she referring to. [G]adia stated, 'Junior, my boyfriend.'... Gadia, in a low tone of voice, stated that it was over her coworker. [G]adia started coughing heavily and started to moan. I then ceased the interview and told her that we will come back at a later time to interview her. [G]adia informed me that she was afraid of Junior and does not want to see him, that she wanted him to go to jail in regards to what he did to her.

For a statement to be admitted under an excited utterance exception to hearsay, most courts have interpreted Columbia Rule of Evidence 803(2) to require: 1) an event or condition startling enough to cause nervous excitement; 2) the statement relates to the startling event; and 3) the statement must be made while the declarant is under the stress of the excitement caused by the event before there is time to contrive or misrepresent. All three inquiries bear on the ultimate question: Whether the statement was the result of reflective thought or whether it was a spontaneous reaction to the exciting event.

It was not an abuse of discretion for the trial court to find the first two requirements, that the event or condition was startling enough to cause nervous excitement and that the statements relate to the startling event, were satisfied in this case. It was not an abuse of discretion for the trial court to find that Gadia being run over by a truck, experiencing life-threatening physical trauma, extensive surgery and intensive medical care was startling enough to cause nervous excitement.

The third requirement that the statement must be made while the declarant is under the stress of the excitement caused by the event consumes the bulk of the contention and analysis in cases applying the excited utterance exception. Courts look at various external factors as indicia of the declarant's state of mind at the time of the statements and no one factor is dispositive. In deciding whether the statement was the product of stress and excitement rather than reflective thought, courts have considered various factors in totality which may include, but are not limited to: the lapse of time between the startling event and the statement, whether the statement was made in response to an inquiry, age/maturity of the declarant, the physical and/or mental condition of the declarant, characteristics of the event, and the subject matter of the statements.

The lapse of time is often a central inquiry to determine whether the declarant spoke under the stress of the excitement caused by the event, but this factor is not dispositive. The inquiry focuses on the psychological impact of the event itself and not upon the contemporaneous nature of the startling event. Based on the totality of the circumstances, statements made hours after the startling event may still fall within the excited utterance exception.

Although not determinative, a statement made in response to an inquiry could bear on whether the statement was spontaneous or deliberative. However, a victim's statement made in response to an inquiry does not, without more, negate its spontaneity as an excited utterance.

Often, a witness' description of the declarant's emotional state is sufficiently weighty in determining whether the declarant's state of mind falls with the excited utterance exception. Describing the declarant's voice, appearance, demeanor, whether the declarant was crying or appeared frightened, is often sufficient to demonstrate that the declarant was in an excited state.

In cases where a declarant has lost consciousness or the ability to speak after sustaining fatal or nearly fatal wounds, declarant's accusatory statement made upon regaining consciousness or recovering the ability to speak is often admissible under an excited utterance exception to hearsay, despite the lapse of time.

Based on the totality of the circumstances, it is reasonable for the trial court to find a six-day delay between getting run over by a truck and speaking to Officer

Nakamura to fall within the excited utterance hearsay exception. Throughout those six days, Gadia was either semiconscious or unconscious and was unable to speak due to her physical condition, medication (painkillers and sedatives), anesthetic drugs and ventilator tube.

Accordingly, we AFFIRM the judgment of the Superior Court.

PT-B: SELECTED ANSWER 1

SUPPORTING MEMORANDUM OF POINTS AND AUTHORITIES

Part I: Any nonverbal statements allegedly made by Gloria Daniel to the police during an interview should be suppressed because it is both inadmissible hearsay and a violation of defendant's constitutional rights.

A. Gloria Daniel's nonverbal statements to the police are not admissible under the excited utterance exception to the hearsay rule because it was not "statement" as defined under the Columbia Rules of Evidence, considerable time had elapsed between the exciting event and the alleged statement, it was in response to repeated inquiry, and Daniel's sedated mental state caused her to no longer be under the stress of the event and able to communicate.

i. Gloria's alleged nonverbal statements to the police are not a "statement" under the law.

Hearsay is a statement, other than one made by the declarant while testifying at the trial or hearing, offered in evidence to prove the truth of the matter asserted. Columbia Rule of Evidence 801(c). A statement is an oral or written assertion or nonverbal conduct of a person, if it is intended by the person as an assertion. CRE 801(a). Here, the police assert that Gloria Daniel nodded her head in response to an inquiry from Officer James as to whether her son Christopher had attacked her. However, the witness herself has indicated that at the time of the questing by Officer James, she was "in deep pain and suffering . . . making it impossible to speak, and therefore, could not have responded to any questions." R. at 13. Furthermore, Gloria was unable to speak for over a month following the attack. R. at 13. Finally, per sworn affidavit of Dr. Nancy Donahue, people with brain injuries have erratic movements of their arms and legs. R. at 7. It is clear from the record that Gloria sustained severe injuries to her head and face. R. at 10. Dr. Donahue avers that it is common for brain injury patients who nod their heads up and down, and that such movements are not intended to convey a "yes" response. R. at 7. Moreover, Dr. Donahue avers that even if a brain-injured person were oriented in time and time, and able to understand, this does not mean that they have any memory of the event that caused the brain injury. R. at 8.

In this case, Gloria suffered an extensive head wound that in all probability will result in her death. She maintains that she did not communicate with Officer James, and to this day has no memory who attacked her. R. at 13. This fact coupled with Dr. Donahue's professional opinion, based on her experience with patients with brain injuries, renders a high probability that Gloria did not make a "statement" as defined under the Columbia Rules of Evidence, and thus, it cannot be admitted under a hearsay exception in any event.

ii. Gloria's alleged nonverbal statements do not fall under the excited utterance exception to hearsay.

Rule 803 of the Columbia Rules of Evidence holds that an excited utterance is an exception to the hearsay rule. An excited utterance is defined as "a statement relating to a startling event or condition made while the declarant was under the stress of excitement cause by the event of condition." CRE 803(2). The Supreme Court of Columbia has interpreted Rule 803 to require: (1) an event or condition startling enough to cause nervous excitement; (2) the statement relates to the startling event; (3) the statement must be made while the declarant is under the stress of the excitement caused by the event before there is time to contrive or misrepresent. See People v. Jackson, Supreme Court of Columbia (2009) at 18. "All three inquiries bear on the ultimate question: Whether the statement was the result of reflective thought or whether it was a spontaneous reaction to the exciting event." Id. The third requirement that the statement must be made while the declarant is under the stress of the excitement caused by event is often the determining factor. Id. at 19. Courts look to various external factors in this regard, including the lapse in time between the startling event and statement, whether the statement was made in response to an inquiry, age/maturity of the declarant, the physical and/or mental condition of the declarant, characteristics of the event and the subject matter of the statements. Id.

First, in this case, it is probable that an attack on Gloria was a startling event and that any statement regarding her attack would relate to that event. However, in weighing the third factors, any nonverbal communication by Gloria to Officer Jackson falls clearly outside the bounds of whether she made the statement under the stress of the event. First, there was a considerable lapse in time in between the attack and when officer Jackson inquired into Gloria's attacker; Gloria was attacked at 12:10 a.m. on August 13. R. at 13. Officer Jackson did not arrive until 12:30 a.m. R. at 9. Furthermore, another ten minutes elapsed before he made the inquiry. R. at 11. This means that half an hour had passed since the attack on Gloria and the inquiry. There is also evidence that the 911 call notifying police of the event came in at 12:43 -- but in any event, there was at least the lapse of the time in between the call plus the ten minutes it took for Officer Jackson to search the house. Courts have held that "the lapse of time is often a central inquiry to determine whether the declarant spoke under the stress of an excitement." People at 19. In this thirty minutes, Gloria had time for "reflective thought" as opposed to a "spontaneous reaction to the exciting event." Id. at 18.

The prosecution will cite People v. Jackson itself as authority that comments made several hours or even days have passed after the startling events can fall within the excited utterance exception. However, this case is distinguishable from People in several respects. First, the witness in People had lost consciousness since the time of the attack or was in a state of semi-consciousness before she awoke six days later and identified her attacker. People at 20. Second, the witness in People actually spoke, and with words identified her attacker. Id. at 19. The Court in People reasoned that where a declarant has lost consciousness, accusatory statements made upon regaining consciousness or recovering the ability to speak is admissible despite the lapse in time. Id. at 19. However, in this case, Gloria was conscious, although seriously injured, upon the arrival of Officer Jackson. R. 10. Furthermore, she was conscious when he made the inquiry. R. 11. Thus, this is not a case where the witness was attacked, became unconscious, and awoke still under the stress of the event. Gloria had ample time to reflect on the attack. Furthermore, the further consideration of the other factors also indicate this fact.

Second, Gloria's alleged nonverbal statement was in response to Officer Jackson's repeated inquiries. Jackson admitted asked Gloria a total of five times who her attacker was: once whether it was a member of her family, another time whether it was her son Jonathon, another time if it was Christopher, two more times to affirm it was Christopher. "A statement made in response to an inquiry could bear on whether the statement was spontaneous," although this fact is not determinative. People at 19. However, Officer Jackson's repeated inquiries gave Gloria substantial time to reflect and answer. Furthermore, this is not the only factor indicating that Gloria's alleged nonverbal communication was not spontaneous and under the stress of the event.

Third, considering the physical/mental state of the declarant factor, the facts reflect that Gloria was given a sedative when the ambulance arrived. First Responder Kevin Robert states that when he arrived on the scene, Gloria was in extreme distress. However, he inserted an IV line to administer a sedative, and states that she responded to the sedative and calmed down. R. at 12. It was only after that that Officer Jackson asked Gloria the identity of her attacker. Thus, Gloria was under the influence of calming and sedative drugs, which directly negates any arguments of a spontaneous declaration. By Robert's own statement, Gloria was calm. Thus, any nonverbal communication could not have been "spontaneous" as required by law.

For these reasons, Gloria's nonverbal communication should not be admitted, as it does not fall under the excited utterance exception to hearsay.

B. Gloria's alleged nonverbal statements should be suppressed as a violation of the Confrontation Clause because the communication was not given during an ongoing emergency and it was obtained by a police officer attempting to procure evidence as opposed to responding to an emergency.

The United States Supreme Court has held clearly held that testimonial statements of witnesses absent from trial have been admitted only where the declarant is unavailable, and only where the defendant has had a prior opportunity to cross-examine. Crawford v. Washington (2004) at [6]. "Statements taken by police officers in the course of interrogations are . . . testimonial." Id. "Statements are nontestimonial when made in the course of police interrogation under circumstances objectively indicating that the primary purpose of the interrogation is to enable police assistance to meet an ongoing emergency." Davis v. Washington, (2006) at 9. "They are testimonial when the circumstances objectively indicate that there is no such ongoing emergency, and that the primary purpose of the interrogation is to establish or prove past events potentially relevant to later criminal prosecution." Id.

Here, Gloria will likely be unavailable for trial. R. at 13. She remains in serious condition and the prognosis for her recovering is not good. R. at 13. This means that any former statement made by Gloria in setting in which she was not cross-examined inadmissible.

Gloria's alleged nonverbal statement was testimonial. The facts reflect that when Officer Jackson arrived at the house, he searched it and the attacker was not inside. R. at 10. Furthermore, as outlined above, nearly forty minutes had passed since the alleged attack and Officer Jackson's inquiry. The record also reflects that an ambulance had arrived and Gloria was receiving medical treatment. There was no indication that an immediate danger was present or that Officer Jackson's questions to Gloria were inquiries made to "enable police assistance to meet an ongoing emergency." Davis at 9. Gloria was being loaded onto the ambulance to receive care from others when Officer Jackson stopped them to ask her questions about the attack based after receiving information from the 911 operator. R. at 11. The only motive Officer Jackson could have had was to obtain relevant evidence to (1) identify the attacker in order to arrest him and (2) preserve the evidence for a later trial.

The prosecution will argue that this case is analogous to the facts of Davis, where a victim made statements to a 911 operator that identified her attacker. Davis at 11. In

<u>Davis</u>, the Court deemed the statements to be non-testimonial for several reasons; first, the victim in Davis was facing an ongoing emergency whereby her attacker was still present when she called 911; second, the statements elicited from the victim were necessary to resolve that emergency so that dispatched officers might know whether they would be encountering a violent felon. <u>Id.</u> at 11 -12.   The record is clear that Gloria's attacker had left -- Peter stated that fact, R. at 15, and Officer Jackson had made sure the house was clear.   Thus, Officer Jackson had no need to elicit the information regarding the identity of Gloria's attacker for his own safety, but rather, it was in order to apprehend him.

Standing alone, procuring the identity of an attacker in a non-emergency situation surely qualifies as testimonial under the tests set forth in <u>Davis</u> and <u>Crawford</u>. The defendant in this case has had no opportunity to cross-examine Gloria regarding this statement; thus, offering this statement after in the likely events that Gloria becomes unavailable would be in violation of the defendant's right to confront the witnesses against him.

Part II. Any transcript or testimony recording concerning the 911 call allegedly made by Peter Daniel should be suppressed, as it is inadmissible hearsay and violates the defendant's constitutional right to confront the witnesses against him.

<u>A. The transcript of Peter's 911 call is inadmissible hearsay, and does not fall under the business record exception as 911 call transcripts are produced to use as evidence at trial.</u>

Hearsay is a statement, other than one made by the declarant while testifying at the trial or hearing, offered in evidence to prove the truth of the matter asserted. Columbia Rule of Evidence 801(c). Columbia Rule of Evidence 803 provided that public records and reports constitute an exception to the hearsay rule if they set forth matters observed pursuant to duty imposed by law as to matters there was a duty to report, excluding however, in criminal cases, matters observed by police officers and other law enforcement and other enforcement personnel. The United States Supreme Court has held that documents kept in the regular course of business activity are not encompassed by the business record exception if the regularly conducted business activity is the production of evidence for use at trial. Melendez-Diaz v. Massachusetts, U.S. Supreme Court (2009) at 14.

Here, the transcript and recording are regularly kept by the police, and consist of observations of ongoing emergencies as presented by conversations between operators and alleged victims. However, such transcripts and recording are expressly forbidden by Rule 803, as they were matters observed by police officers and other law enforcement personnel. "If 911 operators are not themselves law enforcement officers, they may at least be agents of law enforcement when they conduct interrogations of 911 callers." Davis at 9. Accordingly, any matters or conversations had by the 911 operator and subsequently made into the transcript or recording do not fall under the business record exception. In the alternative, were the Court to consider the transcript an exception, the United States Supreme Court has expressly held that "Business and public records are generally admissible absent confrontation not because they qualify under an exception to the hearsay rules, but because . . . they are not testimonial." Melendez at 15. As outlined below, the statements elicited from Peter Daniel from the 911 caller are testimonial and thus subject to the Confrontation Clause, and accordingly, they are nonetheless admissible.

B. The transcript and recording of Peter's 911 call does not fall under the excited utterance exception due to the lapse in time from the attack to the call and the likelihood that Peter was no longer under the stress of the event.

Rule 803 of the Columbia Rules of Evidence holds that an excited utterance is an exception to the hearsay rule. An excited utterance is defined as "a statement relating to a startling event or condition made while the declarant was under the stress of excitement caused by the event or condition." CRE 803(2). The Supreme Court of Columbia has interpreted Rule 803 to require: (1) an event or condition startling enough to cause nervous excitement; (2) the statement relates to the startling event; (3) the statement must be made while the declarant is under the stress of the excitement caused by the event before there is time to contrive or misrepresent. See People v. Jackson, Supreme Court of Columbia (2009) at 18. "All three inquiries bear on the ultimate question: Whether the statement was the result of reflective thought or whether it was a spontaneous reaction to the exciting event." Id. The third requirement that the statement must be made while the declarant is under the stress of the excitement caused by event is often the determining factor. Id. at 19. Courts look to various external factors in this regard, including the lapse in time between the startling event and statement, whether the statement was made in response to an inquiry, age/maturity of the declarant, the physical and/or mental condition of the declarant, characteristics of the event and the subject matter of the statements. Id.

Here, as an initial matter, Peter made clear that the attack not only over, but that his attacker had left and was driving to a location almost three hours away. R. at 14, 15. Thus, it is arguable that he was no longer under the stress of the event or fear of the attacker. Secondly, in the lapse in time between the time of the attack and picking up the phone, Peter had time to "reflect" on what had happened in order to repeat it to the 911 operator. People at 19. The prosecution will argue that Peter was "heav[ily] breathing" when he made the 911 call, indicating that he was stressed from the event. R. at 1. However, first, that was only a characterization of the operator, and second, the record shows that Peter sustained mortal injuries, the pain of which could have caused his heavy breathing as opposed to the stress of the attack. R. at 10. Furthermore, Peter's statements regarding the identity of his attacker were made in response to inquiry from the operator. R. at 15. "A statement made in response to an inquiry could bear on whether the statement was spontaneous," although this fact is not determinative. People at 19.

Overall, the factors weigh against the admission of this testimony as an excited utterance, and the transcripts should be suppressed as inadmissible hearsay.

C. The transcript and recording of Peter's 911 call violates the defendant's right to confront the witnesses against him because the call concerned past events and not an ongoing threat, and the 911 operator elicited statements not to deal with an ongoing emergency but rather to obtain evidence of a past event.

The United States Supreme Court has clearly held that testimonial statements of witnesses absent from trial have been admitted only where the declarant is unavailable, and only where the defendant has had a prior opportunity to cross-examine. Crawford v. Washington (2004) at [6]. "Statements taken by police officers in the course of interrogations are . . . testimonial." Id. "If 911 operators are not themselves law enforcement officers, they may at least be agents of law enforcement when they conduct interrogations of 911 callers." Davis at 9. "Statements are nontestimonial when made in the course of police interrogation under circumstances objectively indicating that the primary purpose of the interrogation is to enable police assistance to meet an ongoing emergency." Davis v. Washington, (2006) at 9. "They are testimonial when the circumstances objectively indicate that there is no such ongoing emergency, and that the primary purpose of the interrogation is to establish or prove past events potentially relevant to later criminal prosecution." Id.

In this case, the transcript shows that Peter called after his alleged attacker had left. R. at 15. Thus, the call related to past as opposed to events that were actually happening. Second, the 911 operator went beyond scope of assisting Peter and instead attempted to identify his attacker for law enforcement purposes. R. at 15. The 911 operator did not ask about the extent of Peter's injuries or give advice on what to do in order to help himself or aid his wife. Rather, the operator instantly began a battery of specific questions meant only to procure evidence and apprehend the attacker. The 911 caller asked for the attacker's name and license plate number. This was not to "enable police assistance to meet an ongoing emergency," but rather to apprehend the attacker. Davis at 9. The facts are clear that the attacker had left Peter's vicinity, and thus he was in no further danger. The only remaining motive of the 911 operator was to procure information "potentially relevant to a later criminal prosecution." Id.

The prosecution will again argue that this case is analogous to Davis. As set forth above, in Davis, the victim calling in was still under attack and facing an ongoing emergency, and the question posed by the operator, namely simply asking her the attacker's name, was necessary to resolve that emergency so that dispatched officers might know whether they would be encountering a violent felon. Davis, at 9, 11-12. The prosecution will further compare the "frantic answers" provided by the victim in Davis to the unintelligible and apparently breathless answers Peter provided. R. at 15-16.

In regard to the first argument, in this case, Peter had made clear that his attacker had left. R. at 15. Thus, there was no need to obtain information regarding the attacker, as dispatched officers would not be "encountering a violent felon" upon their arrival. Davis at 12. The only use of such information is to apprehend the attacker, which is clearly testimonial evidence under Crawford. Furthermore, the operator in this case went beyond the simple question asked by the operator in Davis, which is further evidence that she exceeded the scope of responding to an ongoing emergency. The operator in Davis asked only for the attacker's name. Davis at 9-10. In this case, the operator went so far as to confirm the attacker's model of car and his license plate number. R. at 15-16. Such information is not relevant in responding to what was a medical emergency. As to the second argument regarding the nature of the victim's answers, although Peter's answers are not completely calm, they were made in a safe environment, as his attacker had left. Furthermore, the formality of the so-called interview is only one factor in ascertaining whether a statement is testimonial. As outlined above, there is ample support that Peter's statements were elicited to assist law enforcement in investigating the crime rather than responding to the emergency.

Accordingly, because the comments elicited from Peter by the 911 caller were testimonial, and because he is unavailable and has not been cross-examined, the transcript and recording of the call should be suppressed pursuant to the Confrontation Clause.

Mary Lynch

State Bar # XXXXX

Lynch and Maurer, Attorneys at Law

Avery Park, Columbia

STATE OF COLUMBIA	Criminal Division
v.	CASE NO. 2014-2341
CHRISTOPHER DANIEL	MOTION TO SUPPRESS

MEMORANDUM OF POINTS AND AUTHORITIES

I. The nonverbal statements allegedly made by Gloria Daniel to the police on August 12-13, 2014 should be suppressed because they are inadmissible hearsay, or in the alternative, a violation of Christopher's Sixth Amendment Rights

A. Ms. Daniel's head nods do not fall within any hearsay exception, and thus are inadmissible

Hearsay is a statement offered in evidence to prove the truth of the matter asserted. Col. Rule of Evid. 801(c). A statement is an oral or written assertion or a nonverbal conduct of a person, if it is intended by a person as an assertion. Col. Rule of Evid. 801(a). Hearsay statements are inadmissible unless they fall under an exception to the hearsay rule. Exceptions to the hearsay rule include an excited utterance pursuant to

Col. Rule of Evid. 803(2) and the public records and reports exception under Col. Rule of Evid. 803(8).

In the instant case, Gloria Daniel's (Ms. Daniel's) nods to Officer Tyler James (Ofc. James) did not constitute hearsay because this nonverbal conduct was not intended by her as an assertion. As such, these statements are inadmissible because they are not relevant. Even if these head nods are hearsay, they do not fall under any of the hearsay exceptions. Thus, these statements by Ms. Daniel should be excluded and suppressed.

Ms. Daniel's head nods were not intended by her to be an assertion

Pursuant to Col. Rule of Evid. 801(b) the nonverbal conduct of a person is a statement pursuant to Col. Rule of Evid. 801(c) if the conduct is intended by a person as an assertion. In determining a preliminary question concerning the admissibility of person to be a witness, a court is not bound by the rules of evidence, except those with respect to privileges. Further, when the relevancy of evidence depends on the fulfillment of a condition of fact, the court shall admit it upon the introduction of evidence sufficient to support a finding of the fulfillment of the condition.

Ms. Daniel's head nods were not intended by her to be an assertion. As noted in Dr. Nancy Donahue's affidavit, it is very unlikely, if not impossible, that Ms. Daniel would have any memory of the event that caused the injury. Dr. Donahue states that Ms. Daniel had a serious brain injury. She notes that many people with serious brain injuries have erratic movement of their arms and legs. Indeed, it is noted by paramedic Kevin Robert that Ms. Daniel was moving erratically back and forth, suggesting symptoms consistent with Dr. Donahue's diagnosis.

Even though Officer James asked Ms. Daniel questions prior to asking her if Christopher did this, these preliminary questions do demonstrate that Ms. Daniel intended her nods to be a yes to Ofc. James's questions regarding Christopher. Ms.

Daniel allegedly nodded yes that that one member of her family had been responsible for her injury. She then shook her head no that it was not her son Jonathan. Ofc. James claims that Ms. Daniel then shook her head yes in response that Christopher was responsible for her injuries. Ofc. James further contends that she nodded yes both times after being asked this same question. This repetitive nodding to the same question does not suggest an assertion by Ms. Daniel that she was responding yes to these questions. It is very likely that Ms. Daniel was just repeatedly nodding. Dr. Donahue further notes that there are brain injury patients who may nod their heads up and down, but do not really intend the "yes" response.

Even if Ms. Daniel was oriented and able to follow commands and generally answer questions, this does not mean that she had any memory of what caused her injury. As attested to by Dr. Donahue, even if a brain injured person was oriented and could generally answer questions, it was very unlikely that she would have any memory of the event causing the injury. As such, Ms. Daniel could not have intended her head nods to be an assertion.

Furthermore, in an interview with Ms. Daniel on February 11, 2105, Ms. Daniel confirmed that she "was in deep pain and suffering from a head injury" and could not have responded to any of the questions. She had no recollection of even being asked questions by Ofc. James. She claimed that at no time has she identified who the attacker was. Even though these statements by Ms. Daniel are hearsay statements, the court is allowed to consider them in deciding the preliminary question of whether to admit Ms. Daniel's statements.

Finally, Ms. Daniel was given a sedative by Kevin Robert prior to nodding her head in response to Ofc. James' questions. Mr. Robert stated that Ms. Daniel immediately responded to the sedative and calmed down. A massive head injury combined with a sedative more than likely prevented Ms. Daniel from being able to answer Ofc. James' questions.

All the above mentioned evidence is sufficient to support a finding that Ms. Daniel did not intend her head nod to be an assertion. As such, Ms. Daniel's head nods were not hearsay and cannot fall within any exception. Furthermore, Ofc. James' testimony regarding Ms. Daniel's head nods is not relevant because it does not have any tendency to make any fact in this case more or less true. Thus, Ms. Daniel's head nods should be excluded.

Even if Ms. Daniel's head nods were intended to be an assertion, they are inadmissible hearsay

Even if Ms. Daniel's head nods were intended to be an assertion that Christopher was responsible for her injuries, these nonverbal movements are hearsay statements that do not fall under an exception.

Ms. Daniel's statements are not an excited utterance
Pursuant to Rule 803, a hearsay statement relating to a startling event or condition made while the declarant is under the stress of excitement caused by the event or condition is admissible. *People v. Jackson* (Columbia Supreme Court, 2009) expounded on this exception to the hearsay rule. The court noted that to determine whether a declarant was still under the stress of the event a totality of the circumstances test will be used. Factors include lapse of time, whether the statement was made in response to injury, age/maturity, physical/mental condition, characteristics of the event, and the subject matter of the statements.

The *Jackson* court noted that lapse of time is a central inquiry. Here, more than a number of minutes, perhaps even an hour passed between when Ms. Daniel was injured and when she made her head nods. Ms. Daniel claims that she was attacked at approximately 12:10 a.m. The 911 call from her husband was made at 12:43 a.m. Ofc. James must have arrived after because Peter Daniel was dead when he arrived. Although Ofc. James claims that he arrived around 12:30 a.m., he was approximating the time. Ofc. James claims that he went to clear the house, which took him about 10 minutes. During the search he heard the ambulance arrive. When Ofc. James questioned Ms. Daniel she was placed on the gurney; thus it is likely that Ms. Daniel made the statement at least an hour after the injury. Although in *Jackson*, the court still found that the declarant was under the stress of the event after a week, this was because the declarant had lost consciousness during this week period. Here, if the prosecution claims that Ms. Daniel could respond to questions, the assumption is that she was not unconscious. Thus an hour after an event occurred is enough to no longer be under the stress of the event.

Further the *Jackson* court noted that a response to an injury could make the statement less likely to be under the stress of an event. Here, Ms. Daniel was merely responding with head nods to Ofc. James's yes/no questions. This is distinguishable from *Jackson*. In *Jackson*, the declarant actually provided verbal responses to questions asked of her. Making nonverbal statements to nonverbal questions is more likely to negate spontaneity than nonverbal statements given that nonverbal statements require less effort and thus can be more calculated in response to pointed questions.

Although Ms. Daniel was initially in extreme distress when the ambulance arrived, she was not under this distress when she spoke with Ofc. James. As mentioned above, Ms. Daniel had received a sedative prior to speaking with Ofc. James. Mr. Robert noted that she responded to it and it had calmed her down. Thus, Ms. Daniel was no longer under the stress of an event.

Thus, given that over an hour had lapsed since Ms. Daniel's injury, her head nods were less spontaneous and more calculated to respond to questions, and she was calm after receiving a sedative; it is unlikely that her statements were made under the stress of excitement caused by her injuries.

B. Even if Ms. Daniel's statements are admissible under a hearsay exception, the introduction of these statements would violate Christopher's 6th Amendment rights because these statements are testimonial and Christopher has not had an opportunity to cross-examine Ms. Daniel.

Under the 6th Amendment, a defendant has a right to be confronted with the witnesses against him. See *Crawford v. Washington* (U.S. Supreme Court, 2004). Only testimonial statements cause a declarant to be a witness within the meaning of the Confrontation Clause under the Sixth Amendment. A witness's testimony may only be admitted against a defendant if the witness is unavailable and the defendant has had a prior opportunity to cross-examine the witness.

Ms. Daniel's head nods were testimonial statements

In the U.S. Supreme Court decision *Davis v. Washington* (2006), the Court distinguished testimonial statements from non-testimonial statements. A testimonial statement is that which is made "when circumstances objectively indicate that there is no such ongoing emergency and that the primary purpose of the interrogation is to establish or prove past events potentially relevant to later criminal prosecution." A non-testimonial statement is that which is made "when made in the course of a police interrogation under circumstances objectively indicating that the primary purpose of the interrogation is to enable police assistance to meet an ongoing emergency."

To illustrate the difference between testimonial and non-testimonial statements, the Davis court compared the statement made in *Crawford v. Washington* (2004) with the statement made in *Davis*. In *Crawford*, the declarant's statement was testimonial, whereas the statement in *Davis* was not testimonial. Based on a comparison of these two statements, the court acknowledged four factors relevant to determining if a statement is testimonial. First, whether the declarant was speaking about an event that was actually happening or an event that had already happened. Second, whether the declarant was providing a narrative report or facing on ongoing emergency. Third, the nature of what was asked--whether the questions were intended to resolve a present emergency or rather simply learn what had happened in the past. Fourth, the court looked to the formality between the two interviews. Finally, the court in *Melendez-Diaz* noted that another factor to determine the nature of a statement will be whether it was made in anticipation of litigation. If so, it will likely be considered testimonial.

Based on these factors articulated by the court, Ms. Daniel's statement was testimonial. Like in *Crawford*, a time had lapsed since the event (i.e. the causation of her injuries had occurred.) As noted above, approximately an hour had elapsed. Ofc. James did a sweep of the house and noted that the perpetrator was not present. Thus, when Ofc. James asked Ms. Daniel questions, the perpetrator was no longer at the scene, unlike in *Davis*.

Next, Ms. Daniel was not facing an ongoing emergency. The ambulance had arrived and Ms. Daniel's injuries were being attended to by Mr. Robert. Further, Mr. Robert had administered a sedative that allowed Ms. Daniel to calm down. This is unlike in *Davis*, when the victim was speaking to the 911 operator as she her boyfriend was attacking her.

Additionally, Ofc. James's questions were not intended to resolve a present emergency, but rather simply learn what had happened in the past. The perpetrator had already fled and unlike the 911 operator in *Davis*, here Ofc. James was seeking to confirm what the 911 operator had already told him. He was investigating the validity information conveyed on the 911 call.

Moreover, the environment, although not at a station house, still had formal elements. Ms. Daniel did not provide answers in a frantic manner in an environment that was not tranquil. Rather, she was lying on a gurney and calmly nodding to Ofc. James. Ofc. James was asking a series of questions and likely taking physical or mental notes of her responses. This interrogation had the formality of a police investigation.

Finally, Ofc. James's questions were likely asked in anticipation of litigation. Officers are trained to build up cases and as such he was probably collecting evidence that he knew would be relevant and helpful to the District Attorney. Given the manner in which Ofc James was asking the questions, Ms. Daniel could assume that the her statements would be used at trial.

Considering all these factors, Ms. Daniel's head nods were testimonial.

Although Ms. Daniel is unavailable, Christopher has not had an opportunity to cross-examine her

As noted by the court in *Crawford*, testimonial statement may only be admitted if the witness is unavailable and the defendant has had a prior opportunity to cross-examine the witness. The opportunity to cross-examine a witness at trial is a necessary condition for the admissibility of testimonial statements. (*Crawford*.). Here, Ms. Daniel has passed away, and thus she is unavailable. Christopher, however, has not had an opportunity to cross-examine her. Although Christopher's counsel has interviewed Ms. Daniel prior to her death, this was not a cross-examination at trial. Rather, the interview took place at the Avery Park Hospital. Ms. Daniel was not in a courtroom and her statement was not made under oath.

Thus, Ms. Daniel's head nods cannot be admitted because they are testimonial statements and Christopher has not had an opportunity to cross-examine Ms. Daniel. As such, these statements should be suppressed.

II. The transcripts or testimony recording concerning the 911 call allegedly made by Peter Daniel on August 12-13, 2014 should be suppressed as inadmissible hearsay and a violation of Christopher's Sixth Amendment Rights

A. Mr. Daniel's statements are inadmissible hearsay

As defined above, hearsay is an out-of-court statement that is offered in evidence to prove the truth of the matter asserted. A statement is an oral or written assertion or a nonverbal conduct of a person, if it is intended by the person to be an assertion. Here, the 911 statements made by Peter Daniel (Mr. Daniel) on August 12-13, 2014 are statements that were made out of court. It is anticipated that the prosecution will attempt to offer these statements to show that Christopher was responsible for his injuries and his wife's injuries. These statements however, do not fall under any hearsay exception and thus are inadmissible.

Mr. Daniel's statements are not an excited Utterance
Pursuant to Rule 803, a hearsay statement relating to a startling event or condition made while the declarant is under the stress of excitement caused by the event or condition is admissible. *People v. Jackson* (Columbia Supreme Court, 2009) expounded on this exception to the hearsay rule. The court noted that to determine whether a declarant was still under the stress of the event a totality of the circumstances test will be used. Factors include lapse of time, whether the statement was made in response to injury, age/maturity, physical/mental condition, characteristics of the event, and the subject matter of the statements.

Here, Mr. Daniel's statements were made at least 30 minutes or more after the event that caused his injuries. As noted above, Ms. Daniel stated that the attacked occurred around 12:10 a.m. The call to 911 was placed at 12:43. Thus, this call was not made immediately after the event.

Mr. Daniel's statements are not a Public Records and Reports Exception
Under Rule 803(8), records or reports of public offices or agencies regarding matters observed pursuant to duty imposed by law as to which matters there was duty to report are admissible. There is an exception however that excludes these reports in criminal cases for matters observed by police officers and other law enforcement personnel.

The 911 call is not subject to this hearsay exception. Although it was a report of a public agency, this is a criminal case and as such, the report should be excluded. The 911 operator is a law enforcement personnel. As noted in Davis, although 911 operators are not law enforcement, they may be law enforcement personnel when conducting interrogations over 911 calls. Although the court was analyzing 911 operators with respect to whether a statement was testimonial, the court's logic is relevant here. It shines light on the fact that 911 operators often do question callers in a fashion similar to law enforcement and relay this information to law enforcement to help with an investigation. Here, the 911 caller asked questions that were similar to a police interrogation. The operator asked for the name of perpetrator and asked for the license plate number of the car. Furthermore, the operator relayed the information to Ofc. James, which he used to question Ms. Daniel. Thus, this report cannot be admitted under the public records and reports exception given that it was made by law enforcement personnel.

B. Admitting Mr. Daniel's statements would violate Christopher's 6th Amendment rights

As mentioned above, even if hearsay declaration may be admissible under a hearsay exception, they still may be required to be excluded if they violate a defendant's 6th Amendment rights. As noted by the court in dicta in *Melendez-Diaz*, even if statements are admissible under the business records exception, they can still be inadmissible if they violate the Confrontation Clause. Similarly, even if Mr. Daniel's statements fall into a hearsay exception, they can still be excluded if they violate the Confrontation Clause. Testimonial statements made by an unavailable declarant will not be admitted unless the defendant has had an opportunity to cross-examine the declarant. (*Crawford*)

All Mr. Daniel's statements on the 911 call are testimonial statements

The court in *Davis*, while holding that a 911 call was not testimonial, did not hold that 911 calls are per se non-testimonial. In fact the court noted the 911 call evolved into testimonial statements. After the operator gained the information needed to address the exigency of the moment, the emergency appeared to have ended. When the operator proceeded to pose a battery of questions, the victim's statements were then considered testimonial.

Here, unlike in *Davis*, the entire 911 call consisted of testimonial statements. As Mr. Daniel noted in his phone call, the perpetrator had driven off by the time he placed the phone call. Mr. Daniel was no longer reporting an ongoing emergency. Rather, the operator was reporting an event that had already occurred. The operator did not need information to address the exigency of the moment because there were no longer exigency circumstances since the perpetrator had left. The operator asked a series of questions such as the type and color of car the perpetrator was driving and the license plate number. This was not unlike the structured police questioning that occurred in Crawford. Thus, these statements are testimonial.

In the alternative, the court should find that part of the 911 call consisted of testimonial statements

The court should at least find that the statements Mr. Daniel made after the 911 operator dispatched police officers and an ambulance were testimonial. After police officers and an ambulance were sent to Mr. Daniel, the operator no longer needed to address the exigency of the moment. Rather, as in *Davis*, the operator's questioning took the form of a police interrogation. The names of Mr. Daniel's sons, and the color of the Taurus and the partial license plate number provided are all testimonial statements. These are responses to questions asked by the operator that a reasonable person could expect to be used in court. Given that the injury already occurred these answers do not provide information relevant to stopping an emergency, but seek to find the perpetrator.

Christopher has not had an opportunity to cross-examine Mr. Daniel

Even though Mr. Daniel is unavailable to testify because he has passed away, Christopher has not had an opportunity to cross-examine Mr. Daniel in court under oath. As such, Mr. Daniel's testimonial statements must be excluded.

CONCLUSION

Ms. Daniel's head nods were not intended to be an assertion and as such should be excluded. If the court finds that they were intended to be an assertion, then these statements are inadmissible hearsay as they do not fall under any hearsay exceptions. Even if they did, these statements are testimonial and violate Christopher's 6th Amendment rights, and thus should be suppressed. Mr. Daniel's statements should also be excluded. His statements are not hearsay exceptions and even if they are they violate Christopher's rights under the Confrontation Clause. If the court finds that some of Mr. Daniel's statements are not testimonial (those prior to the police being dispatched), the court should still exclude Mr. Daniel's testimonial statements made in the 911 call. We respectfully request that both Ms. and Mr. Daniel's statements be suppressed.

www.ingramcontent.com/pod-product-compliance
Lightning Source LLC
Chambersburg PA
CBHW081732220526
45468CB00008B/2064